BUILDING ADIRONDACK FURNITURE

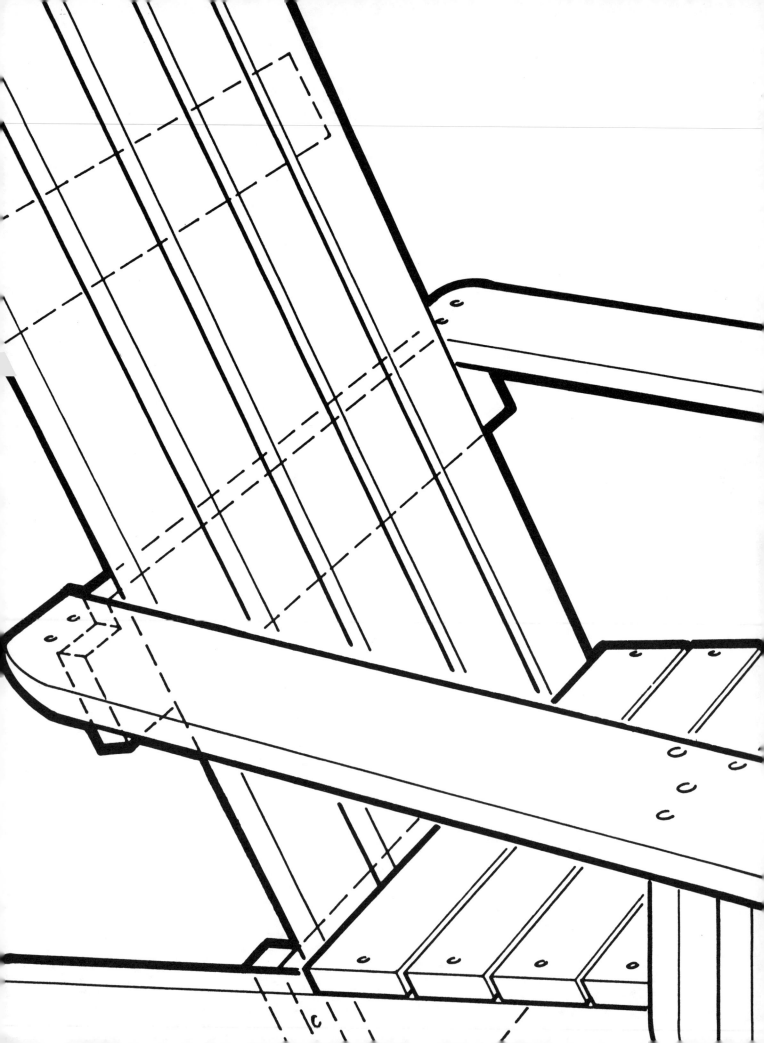

BUILDING ADIRONDACK FURNITURE

THE ART, THE HISTORY, AND THE HOW-TO

JOHN D. WAGNER

WILLIAMSON PUBLISHING COMPANY

CHARLOTTE, VERMONT

John D. Wagner is also the author of
Building a Multi-Use Barn.

ACKNOWLEDGMENTS

This book is for Richard, Gene, Hendrie, and Leita. Thanks for your inspiration.

There are many others to thank as well for their help and support: my dad and mom, and all the members of my family.

I also owe thanks to Clayton, Dave, Marylee, Duffy, JP, and Marnie Lambert. Thanks to Susan and Jack Williamson for supporting the project. Bill Jaspersohn and Tim Healey contributed enormously with editing, photography, and drawings. Thanks to Joseph Lee for the fine design.

I couldn't have written this book without all of your help.

Illustrations by **TIM HEALEY**
Photographs by **BILL JASPERSOHN**
Design by **JOSEPH LEE**
Printing by **CAPITAL CITY PRESS**

Photographs on pages 7-8, 10-16, courtesy of ADIRONDACK MUSEUM, BLUE MOUNTAIN LAKE, N.Y.

Manufactured in the United States
WILLIAMSON PUBLISHING
P.O. Box 185
Charlotte, VT 05445
Telephone: (800) 234-8791

Library of Congress Cataloging-in-Publication Data

Wagner, John D., 1957-
  Building Adirondack Furniture: the art, the history, and the how-to
  / by John D. Wagner.
     p.   cm.
   Includes index.
   ISBN 0-913589-87-X
   1. Outdoor furniture. 2. furniture making I. Title.
 TT197.5.09W34   1994
   684.1'8—dc20   94-30555
                                       CIP

Notice: The information contained in this book is true, complete, and accurate to the best of our knowledge. All recommendations are made without any guarantees on the part of the author or Williamson Publishing. The author and publisher disclaim all liability incurred in connection with the use of this information.

CONTENTS

HISTORY

ONE OF THE
FIRST ADIRON-
DACK CHAIRS,
MADE BY THE
CHAIR'S INVENTOR,
THOMAS LEE,
AROUND 1900 IN
WESTPORT, N.Y.

N O IMAGE OF SUMMER IS COMPLETE WITHOUT THE Adirondack chair. Whether you are squeezing lemonade near a New England seaside, tying trout flies on the deck of your Midwest lake home, shucking pecans on a shady Southern porch, or watching range horses prance in a Western sunset, you are likely to find a cluster of Adirondack chairs nearby. For over 90 years, this chair, with its distinctive, sloped back, inclined seat, and high, wide arms has epitomized summer leisure, while steadfastly evoking the simpler era of its origins.

It doesn't take a Ph.D. to grasp why this chair style endures. Just sit in one and feel the reason why. The Adirondack chair is perhaps the most comfortable piece of outdoor furniture ever invented. That's remarkable, since, traditionally, it is rarely cushioned. In fact, what it offers a weary sitter is usually hard, unadorned wood. Countless comfort buffs, baffled by what makes these chairs so appealing, have engaged in equally countless hours of research over the years to define the chair's charm. You may want to undertake one of these study projects yourself. The procedure is simple: Wait for a hot afternoon, bring along an icy drink and a long novel, pull an Adirondack chair into a patch of shade affording a good view, and sit.

As you let your body conform to that perfect angle defined by the chair's seat and back, imagine for a moment that you live at the turn of the century and are sitting in an original Adirondack chair situated on the rustic porch of one of the great camps in the Adirondack mountains. Here, the staff outnumbers the guests four to one, and the dominant sounds in the air are the padded thuds from a tennis match and the click of mallets and croquet balls on the sprawling lawn below. From the big porch you can see miles of green wilderness blemished only by a distant steamboat's sable plume of smoke and the ripples on a lake from an Adirondack guide boat as it glides home with fresh game from the teeming wilds.

You sip from your drink and open your book. You could sit like this forever.

Though identified with the mountainous region of northeastern New York, the modern-day Adirondack chair may not, in fact, have originated in the Adirondacks. Its parent seems to have been the "Westport chair," named after the town of Westport, N.Y., situated on the southwest shore of Lake Champlain. Similar in shape to the Adirondack chair, though made of slightly

ABOVE

HARRY C. BUNNELL, A CARPENTER FROM WESTPORT, N.Y., CONSTRUCTED THIS CHAIR OUT OF HEMLOCK SOMETIME BETWEEN 1905 AND 1925.

BELOW

PATENT APPLICATION DRAWING FILED BY BUNNELL IN 1904. THE PATENT FOR THE "WESTPORT CHAIR" WAS GRANTED TO HIM IN JULY, 1905.

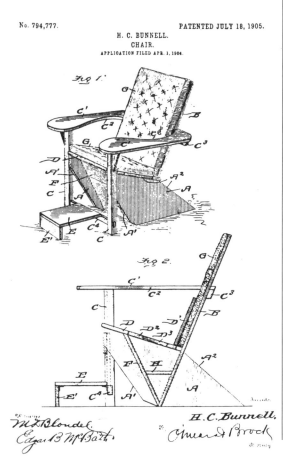

No. 794,777.   PATENTED JULY 18, 1905.

H. C. BUNNELL.
CHAIR.
APPLICATION FILED APR. 1, 1904.

different materials, the Westport chair evolved from the complementary cultures of leisure and improvisation that flourished in the Adirondacks in the late 1800s and early 1900s.

Craig Gilborn, an historian of Adirondack furniture, reports that the Westport chair was first constructed around 1900 by one of Westport's summer residents, Thomas Lee. In letters written years later, Mary Lee, Thomas Lee's niece, recalls the making of the first Westport chair at Stony Sides, the Lee family's summer place on Lake Champlain. "I can vaguely remember," Mary Lee writes, "Uncle Tom's nailing boards together, and getting various members of the family together to sit in [the chair] and tell him when the angles felt exactly comfortable. Then he evolved those great wide flat arms on which you set a cup or glass. Everyone was very much pleased with Uncle Tom's chair and they immediately had two or three more made by a carpenter for the piazza at Stony Sides." Lee's chairs were reportedly still in use on the porch at Stony Sides as late as 1974!

How did the chairs gain such popularity? Where did the name come from? Mary Lee further wrote that Thomas Lee gave one of the chairs to a down-on-his-luck carpenter in Westport named Harry Bunnell. While the two men were out hunting together one day, Harry Bunnell said to Thomas Lee that he had no work to take him through the winter. Mary Lee recalls that Thomas Lee said to him, "I've got a chair that I made that people seem to like very much. I'll lend it to you and you can make a few copies of it, and perhaps you can sell them."

If this story is true, little did Thomas Lee know that he had invented a chair, that, within thirty years, would become a symbol as American as ice cream, as well known as the words to *The Star Spangled Banner*, and nearly as popular as Coca-Cola.

Harry Bunnell not only made and sold the chairs, he may have appropriated the design for his own. Unbeknownst to Thomas Lee, Bunnell filed for a patent on the Westport chair in 1904. He added a few features, including a footrest and storage compartment, but Bunnell's patent drawings essentially depicted the chair Lee built for his family.

The patent for the Westport chair, granted July 18, 1905, is an illustrated description of how to build one, and the patent application's introduction reads, in part: "Be it known that I, Harry C. Bunnell...have invented a new and useful Improvement in Chairs, of which the following is a specification.... The object of the invention is a chair of the bungalow type adapted for use on porches, lawns, at camps and also adapted to be converted into an invalid's chair...a strong durable chair adapted to withstand rough usage and exposure due to weather."

THIS TÊTE-À-TÊTE
CHAIR, MADE OF
BASSWOOD, WAS
BUILT BY HARRY
BUNNELL IN 1925
AT HIS SHOP IN
WESTPORT, N.Y.

By all accounts, Bunnell's business did well, and he went on to make a tête-â-tète version of the chair, as well as a child-size model. For the most part, his sales were to the rustic camps built between 1870 and 1930 in the Adirondacks to the west (Westport is not strictly in the Adirondacks). Bunnell was also probably selling chairs for use by tubercular patients who were coming north out of the cities at that time for the "wilderness cure" at sanatoriums and convalescent homes such as the one at Saranac Lake.

The Westport chair was made of wide boards, not the pine slats you see on most versions of the chair today. In fact, the Westport chair's parts were probably constructed of clear (knot-free) hemlock and basswood, that were then waxed and left un-painted. Ironically, the popularity of the Adirondack region and of the furniture made there may have brought about the very demise of the Westport chair. Production of Bunnell's chairs

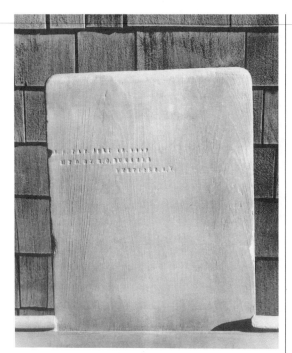

stopped around 1930 because finding the right wood stock for them had become difficult. This seems extraordinary, given the early date. But at that time the Adirondack region's lumber industry was unregulated, and after the great fires of 1903 and 1908, and years of rapacious logging, the amount of Adirondack virgin lumber had been reduced by 1920 to just 4 percent of what originally grew there.

To many, the handwriting was on the wall decades earlier. In 1830, the population of the Adirondack region was 55,000. There followed a large population influx and the dawning of an age marked by unbridled exploitation of the natural resources. As early as 1880, the Adirondacks were considered ruined for logging, hunting, fishing, or raising a family. The population at that time had grown to 113,000 permanent residents. That's 4,000 people *more* than the number of people living there in 1960, eighty years later!

Only after the intervention of determined conservationists and the U.S. government, and with that, the creation of the Adirondack Park, has the region been able to substantially recover its glorious forests and natural habitats.

As for the Westport chair, you may still be able to find some early copies if you scour the attics of Adirondack homes and visit the region's antique shops. You can tell the authenticity of an original Bunnell chair because each is stamped "U.S. PAT. JULY 8, 1905/MFD. BY H.C. BUNNELL/WESTPORT, N.Y." The Bunnell chairs were typically unpainted and left to weather, so if you find an original that is painted, the paint was probably added later. In any event, the original chairs are valuable antiques. A 1967 newsletter, *Know Your Antiques*, by Ralph and Terry Kovel calls an antique Westport chair "one of those rare, truly original furniture designs."

What we know as the modern Adirondack chair probably came into being between 1920 and 1930 as Adirondack carpenters and camp caretakers discovered an ongoing demand for the comfortable Westport chairs, even if the desirable, knot-free boards were unavailable. Ever-resourceful woodsmen and competent builders, they constructed the chairs from pine boards, covering unsightly knotholes with a coat of paint. This approach continues today, with pine boards as the chair material of choice. Typically, an odd number of boards comprises the back support, with one prominent center board establishing the apex of a fan-like arch. A slat seat spans the sloping "stringer" (the part that slopes to the ground in the back), and the front legs rise to support those gloriously wide arms.

Why Westport and Adirondack chairs have remained popu-

LEFT

MODERN-DAY ADIRONDACK FURNITURE RETAINS MANY FEATURES OF THE ORIGINAL MODELS. THIS OAK BENCH, BUILT IN **WILLSBORO, N.Y.,** IN 1986, HAS THE DISTINCTIVE, WIDE ARMS AND SLOPED SEAT CHARACTERISTIC OF EARLY DESIGNS.

BELOW

THIS MODERN OAK CHAIR, BUILT IN **WILLSBORO, N.Y.,** FEATURES A ROLLING SEAT. **ORIGINAL ADIRONDACKS** HAD STRAIGHT, FLAT, SLAT SEATS.

lar has little to do with their adaptability to design materials or ease of construction, though both helped. The fact remains: the chair's design is plainly, undeniably comfortable. As Mary Lee tells us, her Uncle Tom wouldn't finish tinkering with the original chair's design until the "angles felt exactly comfortable." Well, it looks as if he got it right, and, because of him, we've been getting it right ever since.

In the years immediately following Thomas Lee's invention and Harry Bunnell's stint as the Westport chair's builder, the general design for the Adirondack chair travelled far, perhaps first arriving in Cape Cod, Martha's Vineyard, and other points along the New England coast via well-to-do people who had built rustic camps in the Adirondacks, as was fashionable until around 1930. Today, the chair can be found everywhere in North America under various names including Westport Adirondack chair, North Country lawn chair, and garden chair. Recently, while traveling in the American Southwest, I saw a sign near Santa Fe that advertised "Southwest Adirondack chairs." Though you never know

what it may be called next, you can rest assured that the design for any Adirondack chair closely resembles the one Lee invented almost a century ago.

Knowing the Adirondack chair's birth date (around 1900), one might wonder how a chair of such a seemingly clunky, utilitarian design originated during the Victorian age, with its florid, elegant patterns and curlicue styles. In fact, the Adirondack chair is not such an anomaly. But its design must be seen in light of a type of furniture and architectural style, often called American Rustic, that flourished in many parts of the United States, in-

ABOVE

THE ADIRONDACK MOUNTAINS HAVE LONG BEEN A POPULAR AND FASHIONABLE VACATION DESTINATION. IN THIS PHOTOGRAPH, FROM THE 1930s, ADIRONDACK CHAIRS ARE PUT TO THE TEST BY TWO VACATIONING READERS.

cluding the Adirondacks, around the time of the Westport chair's creation. Akin to the Victorian style, American Rustic featured an ornamental use of twigs, rough-cut, log-slab sheathing, applied birchbark, and elaborate, tree-branch woodwork.

The wide, rough-board components of the original Westport chair, though improvised and crude looking, are in keeping with materials that defined American Rustic. Hearkening back to an earlier, English Rustic style, the inventive spirit that emerged in the improvised Adirondack wooden creations—camps, furniture, public buildings—deliberately used unrefined natural materials available at hand. Summing up the style, one Adirondack native wrote, "Trees are as closets from which good woodsmen take whatever they may need."

BELOW
WITHIN A DECADE OF THEIR INVENTION, ADIRONDACK CHAIRS BECAME A TYPICAL PART OF THE SUMMER SCENE.

LEFT
SCHROON LAKE, N.Y., IN THE EASTERN ADIRONDACKS, LOOKS TODAY MUCH AS IT DID 40 YEARS AGO, THOUGH BATHING-SUIT STYLES HAVE CHANGED SOME.

THE CLASSIC
ADIRONDACK CHAIR
IN THE FORE-
GROUND OF THIS
PHOTOGRAPH FROM
THE 1920s IS
SIMILAR TO THE
CHAIR DESIGN
PRESENTED IN THIS
BOOK.

This inventive, American Rustic style was accelerated in the Adirondacks by the engine of leisure that emerged in America after the Civil War. More and more, upper- and middle-class Americans took their holidays in rural settings to escape the bustle and stress of city and suburban living. The quieter country, and the simple rigors of self-dependency to be found there (as popularized by such Transcendentalist writers as Emerson and Thoreau), nurtured an age-old instinct that one fallen too far from nature need only retreat to nature's bosom to rediscover and heal an original innocence. Communing with nature was considered a religious act, and doing so in rustic buildings, on rustic furniture such as Adirondack chairs, it was tacitly believed, could only aid the process.

The American Rustic style also gained support from wealthy industrialists, who, between 1870 and 1930, built what were called "great camps" in the Adirondack region. Webbs, Vanderbilts, Whitneys, Rockefellers, and Harrimans were among those American aristocrats who flocked to the Adirondacks for retreat. Their notion of stylishly "roughing it" trickled down to the masses, and items like the Adirondack chair were the beneficiaries.

And now you can further that Rustic tradition by building your own Adirondack furniture, using the instructions in this book. In upcoming chapters you'll find plans for a traditional

Adirondack chair, table, bench, and leg rest, all meticulously researched and carefully designed. For each piece I have made every effort to reflect and echo the features of Thomas Lee's original chair design. The arms of the Lee chair were level to the ground. In the chair and bench plans presented here, you'll find level arms. In addition, the arms of the original Lee chair were wide—ample enough to support not only your forearms, but a cool drink and a book or two. The arms in this book's chair and bench plans are also wide and ample. Other aspects of this book's chair and bench designs that echo Lee's include the simple, decorative curve along the top of the back and the gentle slope of the back and seat. At the same time, in deference to the occasional do-it-yourselfer, I've opted for simplicity. The furniture presented here is simple to build, and the required materials and tools are readily obtainable. Besides some common pine boards, all you really need to build these pieces are a saw, a drill, a square, sandpaper, and minimal elbow grease. Keeping the design, materials, and tools as simple as possible reflects, I hope, the original Adirondack furniture-making tradition. As you cut and sand your first boards, think how someone, years ago, with common tools just like yours, did what you're now doing, with the same goal of honest comfort honestly achieved. Good luck!

BELOW

PICTURED HERE ARE THE TABLE, BENCH, LEG REST, AND CHAIR PRESENTED IN THIS BOOK. THE CHAIR AND BENCH RETAIN MANY OF THE ORIGINALS' CLASSIC FEATURES: WIDE ARMS, A SLOPED, FLAT-SLAT SEAT AND HIGH, SLOPING BACK.

WHAT KIND OF WOOD SHOULD YOU USE?

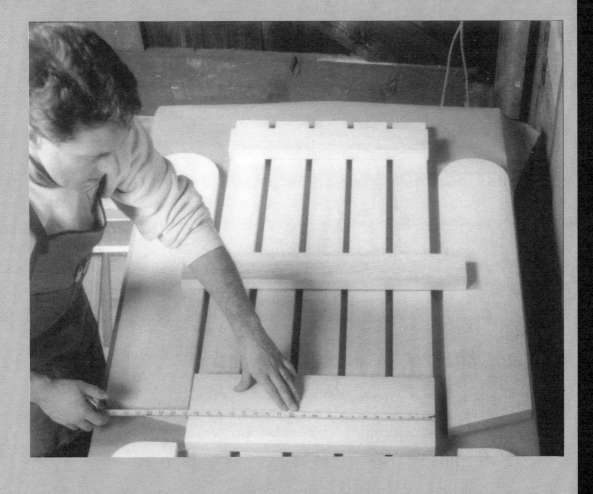

WOOD

HEORETICALLY, YOU CAN BUILD YOUR furniture out of any kind of softwood or hardwood you want. But some wood types are sturdier and last longer than others. In fact, some grades of the *same* wood species last longer than others. When choosing wood, here's what to consider.

■ HARDWOOD VS. SOFTWOOD

There are two types of wood: hardwood and softwood. Hardwood (from trees that lose their leaves) is more expensive, because it grows slowly, lasts longer, has great strength and beautiful grain patterns. The most common hardwoods are oak, maple, and walnut. Birch, white ash, cherry, and mahogany are also popular.

Softwood (from evergreen trees) is less expensive. When rough milled, it is used in house framing. When finished it makes terrific moldings, doors, and cabinets. The most common softwoods are different species of fir and pine. But redwood and Western red cedar are fine woods for their natural resistance to decay.

■ PLAINSAWN VS. QUARTERSAWN

Lumber mills cut logs two different ways, and, as a result, the wood has different properties. "Plainsawn" boards are cut from the log like cheese slices. A band saw cuts the full length of the log, slicing off boards as wide as the log. With quartersawn wood, the log is first cut in quarters. Boards are cut from the quartered sections.

Quartersawn wood, with its tight grain patterns, is more expensive. It weathers better, has spectacular grain patterns, and doesn't shrink, twist, cup, check, or split as much as plainsawn wood. But many lumberyards don't regularly carry quartersawn wood. In fact, you may have to special-order it.

Plainsawn wood is the most common wood out there, and it is what you get unless you specifically request something different. It's perfectly good wood. In fact, some people prefer plainsawn pine boards' grain patterns to quartersawns' patterns.

■ MOISTURE

Wood should have approximately the same moisture content as the air around it. Newly-cut wood has a high moisture content, and it is dried in one of two ways before it gets to you. It can be *air dried*, which doesn't cost the lumberyard much, because they just set the boards out in the open air. Or it can be actively heated, or *kiln dried* ("kd") in a controlled-temperature kiln. Most premium hardwoods and softwoods are kiln dried, driving up their cost, but insuring a more stable product.

■ GRADING

Both softwood and hardwood are graded for appearance and strength. For **softwoods**, the lumber falls into three basic categories: *boards*, *timber*, and *framing lumber*. For our Adirondack furniture projects, we want boards. There are subcategories: The boards will be either *appearance grade* or *general purpose*. We want appearance grade, which itself breaks down into four subcategories: *select, finish, paneling,* and *siding*. Select is the best and siding is the worst. What you choose will depend on your budget and what the wood looks like when the lumberyard person pulls some samples from the stack for your inspection.

For **hardwoods**, there are four grades: *FAS* for *first and second,* followed by *No. 1 common,*

PLAINSAWN LUMBER   QUARTERSAWN LUMBER

No. 2 common, or *No. 3 common.* Nos. 2 and 3 common grades will take a lot of work to use in furniture. You'll have to over-order the quantity and cut out defects before getting good, usable wood. No. 1 common is adequate quality. For budget hardwood users, this is the grade you should buy.

If you want the best hardwood, FAS grade is the premium choice. But within that grade there are other subcategories. There is *clear FAS,* which means completely knot-free. Or, you can get *FAS with one clear side,* which means only one side of the wood will be knot-free.

FAS is not perfect wood by any means. The grading permits some checks and splits to pass muster, but it is the premium wood of choice if you are going to use a hardwood.

On the lumber yard's list of available woods, you may see a designation *S2S* or *S4S.* This simply indicates the number of sides of the board that are finished. Boards with an S2S designation will have rough edges and two sides finished. S4S will have the edges and sides finished.

■ THE IDEAL CHOICES

Top of the line choice? Ideally, for softwoods, the lumber of choice is *kiln-dried, quartersawn, clear select Western red cedar or redwood*. This will provide the highest quality, knot-free, tight-grained boards. (Western red cedar and redwood are the best species because they have natural preservatives and, practically speaking, last forever.) But when you get to the cash register, *sit down!* This will save you from *falling down* when you see the total price. Paradise ain't cheap, and you'll learn that fast when you pay well over $100 for just one chair's worth of wood.

So, let's get more realistic. Given that most of us don't actually print money, a better softwood choice is *select pine*. Just go into your lumberyard and ask for it by name. This is a high-quality product. It will cost you a chunk of change, but you will get some seriously nice-looking wood. As the wood is pulled off the lumberyard rack, carefully examine it and refuse wood that has blemishes, such as gouges, packing-strap marks, or splits. Don't be embarassed to refuse bad lumber. Lumberyard clerks are used to people selecting the best wood, even among premium grades.

Ideally, for hardwoods, the choice of lumber is kiln-dried FAS (S4S) maple or oak. This will make a *gorgeous* piece of furniture. Here too, you will pay a high price for this premium grade.

Let's get realistic here, too. If you really want a hardwood, but FAS is too costly for you, ask to look at a stack of No. 1 common and see if you can live with it. With a little cutting, sanding, and careful planning (so knotty wood is turned away from the seat, back, and arms of the chairs), you may be able to find some nice pieces from what you buy. You may even want to look at No. 2 common.

■ ARE YOU GOING TO PAINT IT ANYWAY?

Only buy premium wood if you are going to put a natural (stain or oil) finish on the wood. Don't spend lots of cash on wood that you will cover with paint. Since all higher grades of wood are strong enough for our furniture, most of what you are paying for in premium woods is appearance.

If you are going to paint, a *panel grade* softwood, such as Douglas fir or southern yellow pine, when sanded carefully, will look great. High-priced wood underneath a paint job is unnecessary.

For hardwoods...well, you'd be a fool to build with a hardwood and then paint it. But No. 2 common, sanded and painted, will look just fine.

■ WHAT THICKNESS OF WOOD TO USE

The ideal wood to use for our furniture projects is $5/4$ (said "five quarter"). This is a board that measures 1 1/4 inches (five quarter inches) before it's planed at the mill. When $5/4$ finally gets to you, it's 1 1/8 inches thick. These boards are very sturdy, and they won't bow under normal circumstances.

If you are not finicky about your Adirondack furniture, and you just want to bang together some serviceable (though nicely designed) lawn chairs, you can use regular 2x construction grade lumber. Run-of-the-mill 2x stock will serve well if you are not choosy about looks and are willing to select out the knotty wood. Again, don't hesitate to be fussy at the lumberyard.

THE TOOLS WE'LL USE FOR OUR FURNITURE MAKING are few and simple. There's no need for elaborate router setups, or jigs, mortises, or plate joiners. We'll take a basic approach and assemble our furniture with screws. If you want, you can go to a more advanced woodworking book and learn to use more professional woodworker's tools. But for our purposes, we'll go with the basics.

Below are descriptions of the power tools you might like to use for the projects, but frankly, you can build this book's furniture with a handsaw, a jigsaw, a screwdriver, and a drill, along with such marking tools as a compass, square, and tape measure. The power tools I'm talking about here will make the job easier, surely, but you don't necessarily need them to build this furniture.

■ CHOP SAW

A *chop saw* loaded with a *finish* or *combo* blade is the ideal tool for cutting our boards to the proper length. It gives a good, square cut, and the saw setup is easy and relatively safe.

A chop saw can also cut the angles on the front end of our stringers. If you own a chop saw, great. It will make things easier. If not, that's O.K., too. You can make the cuts you need with a handsaw and bevel square, or your can do rough cuts with a circular saw and final clean cuts with a table saw.

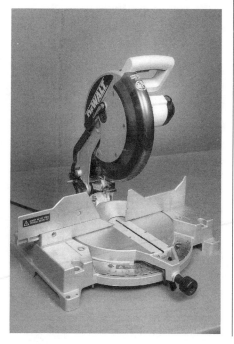

■ TABLE SAW

A table saw is very handy for a variety of woodworking projects, and ours are no different. Any good table saw will do the job, but it has to have a miter gauge, so we can cut a couple of crosscut angles. The ideal blade: An *80-tooth ATB blade*.

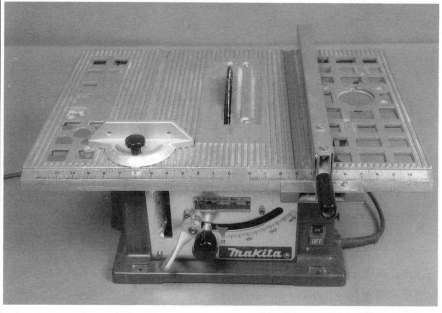

■ JIGSAW AND SABER SAW

For cutting those nicely rounded parts of the chair (the arch around the back, both ends of the arms, and the back of the stringers), we will need a *jigsaw* (also called a *saber saw*). This type of saw can cut curves well because the blade is thin and doesn't bind as you follow a curved line. Use a *finish blade* (a blade with a higher number of teeth per inch than a *rough blade*).

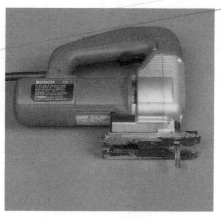

■ SANDER

We'll be doing a bit of sanding, both before and after assembly. Unless you really want *more* hardship in your life, buy, borrow, or rent an electric sander. It will make the sanding enormously easier. Any kind of sander will do, really. I prefer a *palm sander* because it's light and easy to manipulate. You may prefer a *belt sander* or a *pad sander*. It's up to you. It will be very handy to have a belt sander for shaping the rounded parts of the chair after we've made jigsaw cuts. Overall, if you are watching your budget, use a palm or pad sander, because the sheets for them are cheaper than a belt sander's belts.

Most important is the kind of sandpaper you use. For early sanding, use #100 to #120 sandpaper, and for finer finish sanding, use a #220 sandpaper. Optimally, use *garnet* sandpaper. This is the reddish-brown or amber-colored sandpaper (not the black or deep blue). Garnet gives the softest finish because the tiny garnet sanding grits are blocky and attached to the paper backing with animal-hide glue that softens with the friction heat generated when you start to sand.

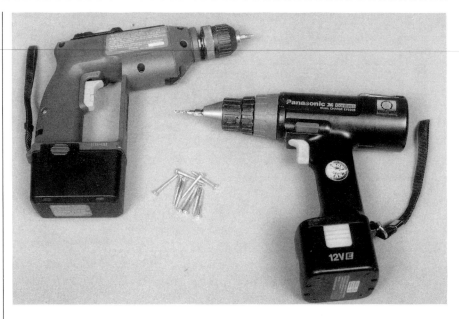

■ DRILL

Use a *variable speed drill* for these projects. Two drills will make drilling even more convenient. One drill can be dedicated to driving screws, and the other can be loaded with a *countersink bit* for predrilling (more later).

What's the countersink for? We will be using #8 *flathead wood screws.* Since we don't want the screw heads flush with the top of the boards, we will "countersink" them, so they sit below the surface of the wood. When predrilling the screw holes, the countersink reams out a slightly wider hole at the surface of the wood so the screw head can be recessed. To do this predrilling, we need a #8 *countersink drill bit.*

■ SCREWS

Use *flathead-type,* 1 ½-inch, #8 *wood screws.* Should they be stainless steel? Well, zinc-plated (the standard silvery kind of screw) work fine—but caveat emptor. They cost about 13 cents each, and they are soft. If the screw stalls in the wood as you drive it, you will likely strip the head. Stripped screws can be a nightmare if you ever have to take them out, or if they strip before they're fully driven. Stainless steel screws, on the other hand, are more durable and won't easily strip. Their drawback? Cost—almost double the cost of zinc-plated screws.

If you are careful about not stripping screw heads, standard zinc-plated screws will work fine. If these are your first woodworking projects, and you don't have much experience driving screws, get stainless steel screws. They're more forgiving.

■ HAND TOOLS

You'll want a nice selection of hand tools ready. Here are some basics: A Phillips screwdriver (the kind with the tapered, cross-shaped drive head); a hammer; a razor-sharp, 1-inch wood chisel; a small combination square (or speed square); and a protractor for marking angles. Have a couple sharp pencils on hand, too.

For drawing larger curves, we will use a pencil on the end of a string. For the curves on the arms and stringers, use a compass that has a pencil mounted on it. (If you have children, check their art supply box; you'll probably find a compass in there.)

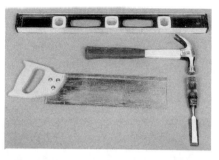

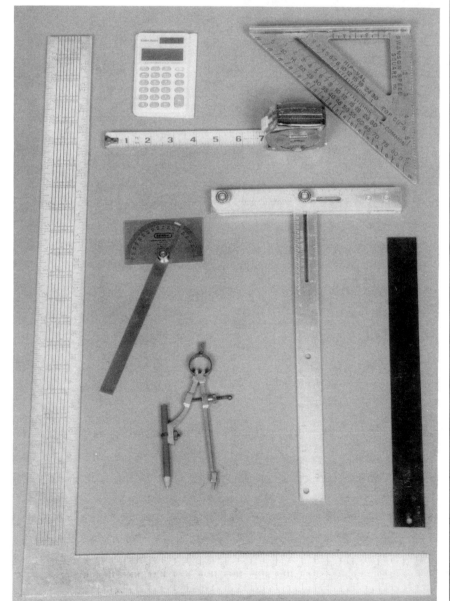

■ EYE AND EAR SAFETY

Never make any saw cut without ear and eye protection. Sure, you may be tough, but a particle in your eye can be very distracting and easily cause you to lose concentration on the saw blade. Not to mention the possible permanent eye damage you could incur. Always wear eye protection.

Though hearing loss is incremental, you can easily damage your ears with the noise these woodworking machines give off. Plus, screaming noise is distracting and aggravating, especially a full day of it. Ear protection makes for a safer work environment, so get it and wear it.

Another tip: Always eat a balanced diet when you are working around power tools. Don't load up on sugars or caffeine. While on the job take food breaks so your blood sugar doesn't drop. You lose your concentration when you are tired or when your energy fades during long time lapses between meals. Most accidents seem to happen either early or late in the day.

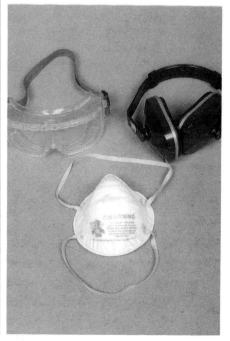

CUTTING

WITH BASIC WOODWORKING TOOLS AND MINIMAL WOODWORKING SKILLS, THIS ADIRONDACK CHAIR CAN BE BUILT IN AN AFTERNOON.

A WORK SURFACE

FOR CUTTING AND ASSEMBLING YOUR Adirondack furniture, use a stable, flat, level wooden surface. Ideally, you want a surface you can circumnavigate easily and kneel on from time to time. If you don't have a woodshop work-table, use a picnic table covered with a sheet of cut-to-fit plywood.

Never work directly on concrete or dirt, because when you kneel on the boards to hold them together as you drive screws, you force grit into the wood, ruining the finish.

LEFT

THIS ADIRONDACK
BENCH IS ESSEN-
TIALLY IDENTICAL
TO THE CHAIR
PICTURED ON THE
FACING PAGE, BUT
WITH A WIDER SEAT
AND BACK.

CHAIR AND BENCH SIMILARITIES

FOR THE ADIRONDACK CHAIR AND ADIRONDACK bench (and parts of the stool, if you make one), many of the components have the exact same dimensions. For instance, the stringers and arms for the chair are identical to those for the bench. In fact, the bench is exactly like the chair, except that the seat and back are wider, requiring more or longer slats.

The descriptions that follow on how to cut curves and angles may apply to the chair, bench, and stool.

If you are making the chair, bench, and stool, you may want to cut the angles all at once, and then set up for and cut all the curves at the same time.

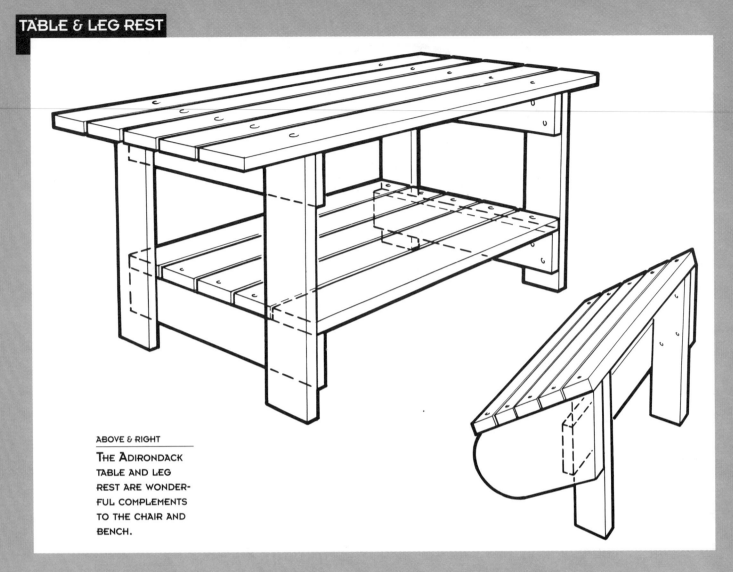

ABOVE & RIGHT

THE ADIRONDACK TABLE AND LEG REST ARE WONDER-FUL COMPLEMENTS TO THE CHAIR AND BENCH.

CUTTING AND PREPARING THE WOOD

DEPENDING ON THE QUALITY OF THE WOOD YOU buy, it probably makes sense to nip 1 inch off the factory ends of the boards before you use them. Nipping off an end starts you with a good, square cut (don't depend on a factory end for square). Plus, it removes any gouges, paint, or grade stamps.

The cut lists for each project show you what lengths of wood to buy. You'll have to determine the wood grade you want, with respect to your budget and the kind of quality you want to end up with (see page 20).

Once you have your wood in hand, use the cutting diagrams supplied in this book to cut your pieces to length. You can use a handsaw to make these cuts, but it's just a lot of work. A circular saw, on the other hand, won't do for this kind of fine work. The blade is too erratic and will not cut a clean line. Ideally, use a chop saw with a finish or combo blade for these cuts. It's a good, safe tool that can cut precisely square and angled lines.

To mark your cuts, use a speed square or combination square. If you are using a handsaw, be sure to stabilize the board you are cutting. If you are using a chop saw, snug the boards up tight against the saw's fence before bringing the blade down. This will insure square cuts.

Marking and Cutting Curves

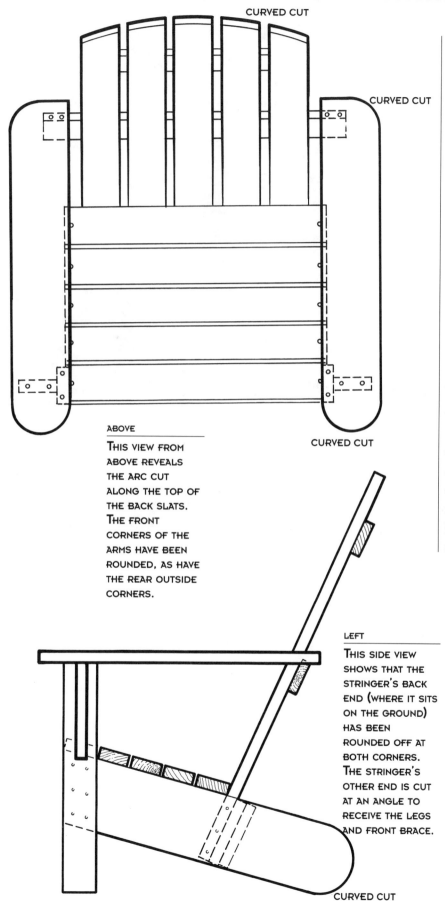

CURVED CUT

CURVED CUT

CURVED CUT

ABOVE

THIS VIEW FROM ABOVE REVEALS THE ARC CUT ALONG THE TOP OF THE BACK SLATS. THE FRONT CORNERS OF THE ARMS HAVE BEEN ROUNDED, AS HAVE THE REAR OUTSIDE CORNERS.

LEFT

THIS SIDE VIEW SHOWS THAT THE STRINGER'S BACK END (WHERE IT SITS ON THE GROUND) HAS BEEN ROUNDED OFF AT BOTH CORNERS. THE STRINGER'S OTHER END IS CUT AT AN ANGLE TO RECEIVE THE LEGS AND FRONT BRACE.

CURVED CUT

FOR THE ADIRONDACK CHAIR AND bench, there are four places you'll cut curves with your saber saw or jigsaw: the arches at the top of the back slats; the rounded ends of the stringers (where they rest on the ground); and both ends of the arms (see drawings on this page). Oh, and one note on sanding these curved cuts. No matter what curved part of the chair you are cutting with the saber saw, you'll find these saws leave rough edges on the end grains. They can be sanded out with a palm sander. But the tool of choice for this task is a belt sander. Not only does it buff the end grain, it also helps to shape and smooth the bumps and irregularities that saber saws inevitably leave behind.

Back to marking and cutting curves: We will draw in the arches at the top of the back slats after the chair is assembled. But the curves for the arms and stringers should be cut before the furniture is assembled.

■STRINGERS

L<small>ET'S START WITH THE STRINGERS</small>. R<small>EMEMBER, WE ARE ONLY</small> cutting curves at one end of each stringer, the end where it touches the ground.

If you don't want to get fancy, you can draw these curves using a coffee can as a template. Hold the curved can to the stringer edge until it looks good to your eye and trace a curved line. Then, break out your jigsaw for the cut.

Or, you can mark the curves with a compass.

For all our curves, we are going to establish a radius that is one-half the width of the board. This makes for an elegant curve. Whether you are cutting the arms or the stringers, your first step is finding the center of the board. For the stringer, which is a 7 1/8-inch-wide board, measure in 3 1/2 inches (close enough to half). Make a light pencil mark. Then, measure back from the end of the board 3 1/2 inches by running your measuring tape along the center of the board. Where the 3 1/2 inch mark from the end meets the 3 1/2 inch mark at mid-board, make a mark. This is where you'll place your compass needle (see above).

How wide should you spread the arms of your compass for drawing the stringer curves? You probably guessed it: 3 1/2 inches. Place your needle in the board's center, 3 1/2 inches back from the board's end. Swing the compass so the pencil draws a curved line from board edge to board edge. Then cut along this line with your saber or jigsaw.

ABOVE

B<small>Y MEASURING IN</small> HALF A BOARD'S WIDTH AND MEASURING BACK FROM THE BOARD END THAT SAME HALF-BOARD DISTANCE, YOU CAN ESTABLISH WHERE TO PLACE YOUR COMPASS POINT IN ORDER TO DRAW AN ELEGANT CURVE.

ABOVE

C<small>URVED CUTS</small> MADE WITH A JIGSAW WILL NEED SOME SANDING TO TAKE OUT THE SAW-BLADE MARKS.

RIGHT

F<small>OR YOUR</small> FURNITURE'S ARMS AND STRINGERS, USE A COMPASS TO DRAW A HALF CIRCLE WHOSE RADIUS IS HALF THE WIDTH OF THE BOARD. T<small>HE JIGSAW</small> WILL CUT ALONG THIS CURVED LINE.

COMPASS

CENTERLINE

ABOVE

WHEN USING A JIGSAW, CANTILEVER THE BOARD YOU ARE CUTTING OVER SCRAP BLOCKS TO ACCOMMODATE THE SAW BLADE.

LET'S MARK AND CUT CURVES ON THE ARMS. START with the front of the arms. Since the 5/4 x 6 arm board is actually 5 ½ inches wide, let's draw a curve that has a radius of half that, or 2 ¾ inches. That radius will create a curve very pleasing to the eye. To draw it, find the center line of the board (it will be 2 ¾ inches in from either side). Then, measure 2 ¾ inches back from the board end. Place your compass needle at the intersection of these two half-board widths. Swing your compass so the pencil draws a curved line, from board edge to board edge.

For the back of the arms, where they attach to the middle back brace, we will draw just one curve, on the outside of the arm. The inside of the arm remains square. The square part of the arm will be screwed into the middle back brace. So, find each board's midpoint, then measure back 2 ¾ inches from each board's end, place your needle, and draw a curved line on the outside of each board.

CUTTING ANGLES

■STRINGERS

LET'S CUT THE ANGLE ON THE FRONT OF THE stringer. The stringer tilts up as it runs from the ground to the chair's front legs. The angle on the front of the stringer will determine the incline of the seat. A comfortable incline for me is between 75 and 80 degrees. (The 75-degree angle will give you a slightly steeper seat.) With your protractor, mark an angle that begins in one corner of the square end of the stringer. Let's make it 75 degrees. Draw a line.

Now, let's cut it. If you have a chop saw, set it to 75 degrees, hold the stringer board square to the saw guide and make a cut, using the line you just drew as your guide.

If you are using a table saw, set your miter gauge to 75 degrees and run your stringer through. For handsaw users, just cut along the guide line you just drew.

Make this identical cut for the chair and bench stringers. The stool stringers will be cut at 60 degrees.

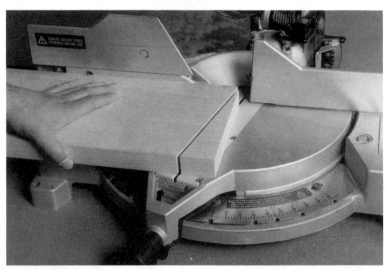

ABOVE

USE A PROTRACTOR TO MARK ANGLED CUTS, SUCH AS THIS ONE ON THE FRONT OF THE STRINGER.

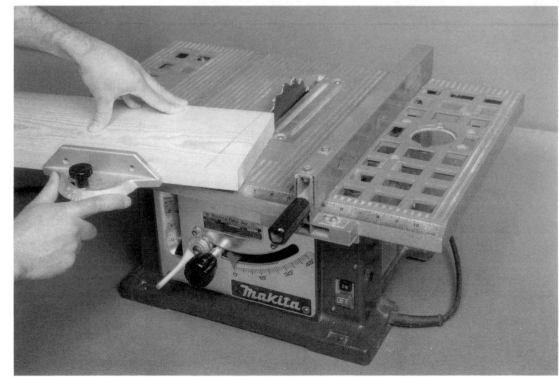

RIGHT

A TABLE SAW WITH A MITER GAUGE SET TO THE DESIRED ANGLE MAKES SHORT WORK OF ANY BOARD. BUT BE CAREFUL OF BINDING AND KICK-BACK.

5° BEVEL

5° BEVEL

ARM SUPPORT

CHAIR OR BENCH LEG

ABOVE

FOR SLOPED ARMS, BEVEL THE TOPS OF THE FRONT LEGS AND ARM SUPPORTS AND ACCOUNT FOR THE SLOPE WHEN POSITIONING THE MIDDLE BACK BRACE.

THE ORIGINAL ADIRONDACK CHAIR HAD ARMS that were level, parallel to the ground. But some people prefer arms that slope down from the front of the chair to the back. We are going to build a chair and bench with level arms. But here's an optional item. If you want to slope the arms of your chair or bench, make a 5-degree-angle cut (called a *bevel*) on the top of the chair or bench's front legs. Cut the top of the arm braces at the same angle.

When you install the middle back brace, you must account for this arm slope by lowering the middle brace on the back by 1 1/8 inches for every 5 degrees of bevel. (You can slope you arms farther, with a 10 degree bevel, and by moving your middle back slat down 2 1/4 inches. But 5 degrees is a common and comfortable slope.)

REMAINING CUTS ▣

THE REMAINING CUTS FOR THE CHAIR, BENCH, stool, and table are all square cuts. That is, you simply mark the boards with your square and cut them to the proper length with your chop saw, handsaw, circular saw, or table saw. If you would like to add some other fancy cuts, see pages 38-39 on fancy cuts.

SANDING

After you have the boards cut to length, use #100 or #120 sandpaper, and sand all the surfaces and ends of the wood. Be careful not to round off the edges of the wood (unless you want that kind of look). After you've made thorough, multiple passes with the #100 sandpaper, go over all the wood again with #220 sandpaper.

Do a thorough sanding job *now*, particularly along the back-slat and seat-slat edges, which won't be accessible once the chair is assembled. Overall, after the chair is assembled, sanding in corners or where boards meet will be difficult, and you'll have to do it by hand. Better to let the machine do the work now.

When the boards are all sanded to your satisfaction, you're ready for assembly.

LEFT

Sand boards before beginning furniture assembly. Sanding afterwards is more difficult.

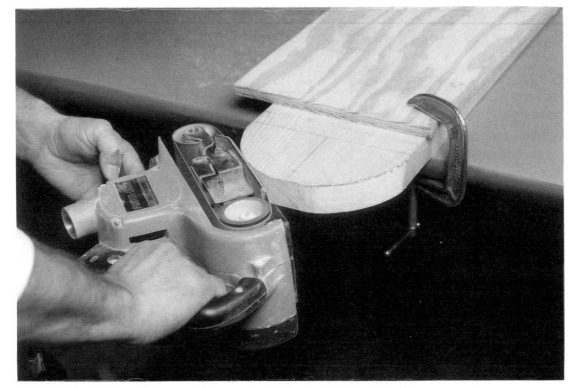

LEFT

A belt sander is an excellent tool for rounding off curves and taking out jigsaw blade marks. But first, clamp the wood securely in place.

You don't have to glue joints when assembling your chair. In fact, if you ever have to take your chair apart (i.e. if you ever have to remove the arms to fit it through a door), you'll be happy you didn't glue. But gluing makes for a sturdy connection: the furniture won't be held together just by the strength of the screws; you'll have the extra bond of the glue.

There are three kinds of glue you can use. The most common is *yellow glue* (also called *carpenter's glue*). It's especially good for open-grain pine, but it will serve you well no matter what kind of wood you use.

A better joint glue is *quick-drying epoxy resin.*

It's a bit more expensive, strong-bonding, and good for any kind of wood. Slower-drying epoxy resin will do just as well and is somewhat cheaper. But it sometimes takes 24 hours to cure.

The best glue to use, (and, naturally, the most expensive), is *resorcinol formaldehyde resin* (called, simply, resorcinol). It's used in marine (boat) work and is very durable on outdoor furniture. It's a bit messy when you mix it, because it's two-part—you mix a fine power and a syrupy goo—and you have to scrape it up to apply it.

The choice of glue is up to you. For best results, use quick-drying epoxy resin.

BELOW

Some basic glue choices: yellow "carpenter's glue," two-part epoxy resin (tubes), and two-part resorcinol (cans).

RIGHT & BELOW

Gluing wood joints that will also be screwed together greatly increases the joints' strength. Here resorcinal is troweled on (above), and boards are laid in place to be screwed down (below).

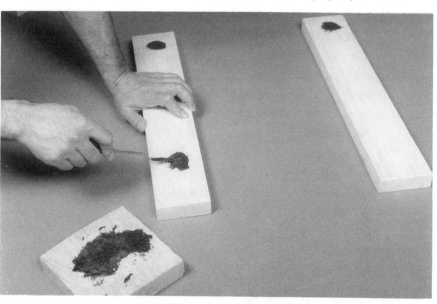

GETTING FANCY

THERE ARE LOTS OF PLACES on your Adirondack chair and bench where you can get fancy with some curved cuts that can really add character. The seat can be given a rolling curve, the stringer can have a curve along its bottom edge, and the front brace can be cut along the bottom edge to match the curves on the top of the back slats or to reflect the curve of the rolling seat. You may also want to give your chair's back an ergonomic contour so that it wraps around you slightly.

In this section, we'll look at some different ways to dress up the seat and front brace. If you want back-slat cutting techniques and patterns, flip ahead to chapter 9. Please note, however, that some of the techniques covered here for measuring, drawing, and cutting circles can be used to cut the back slats, so it wouldn't hurt to read this chapter simply to expand your options.

■ A FANCY ROLLING SEAT

For starters, let's look at how to make a seat that rolls or curves. Look at the drawing below to see what I mean. To make a seat that fancy, you really only have to make two saber-saw cuts, one on each stringer. But then you may have to adjust the width of your seat slats. (The 5/4 x 4s may be too wide for a curve with a radius this severe.) I'll explain how to solve the seat-slat width issue in a moment. First, let's look at how to make the rolling cut.

How do you mark for this rolling seat? Essentially, the curved line for a rolling seat is a tiny segment of a large circle (see above). To fit the slats, we will flatten this

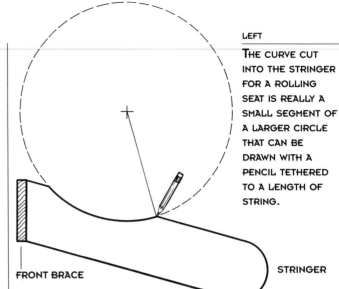

LEFT

THE CURVE CUT INTO THE STRINGER FOR A ROLLING SEAT IS REALLY A SMALL SEGMENT OF A LARGER CIRCLE THAT CAN BE DRAWN WITH A PENCIL TETHERED TO A LENGTH OF STRING.

FRONT BRACE   STRINGER

"circle" where it intersects the stringer near the front. But let's draw the circle first.

Lay your stringer down flat on the work surface. Now take a length of string, (say 2 feet or so) and, tapping a nail halfway into your work surface, establish a "center" to a circle that will be drawn when a pencil swings around the nail at the limit of the string.

Once you've established the center of the circle, slide the stringer into the circle so that just a small segment of the circle falls on the stringer. As you pull the pencil and string taut, sketch lightly on the stringer. Do you like the "roll" line it draws? No? Then adjust the length of string until you get a line to your liking. Be sure that the line you

draw does not go behind the 18-inch mark where the back slats of the chair or bench will be attached. And be sure you have enough flattened area up front—say 4 to 6 inches—to support the front of your legs comfortably when you sit.

When you like the "roll" line, darken it so you can cut along it with your saber saw. Then, using freehand, a string and pencil, or an available circular template such as a garbage can lid, draw an opposing curved line where you want the line to flatten toward the front (see drawing at left).

Once you have one stringer cut, use it as a master stringer guide for cutting other stringers.

Don't like the string and pencil idea? Well, you can freehand this

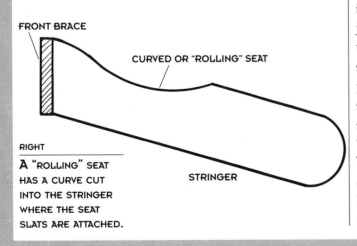

FRONT BRACE

CURVED OR "ROLLING" SEAT

STRINGER

RIGHT

A "ROLLING" SEAT HAS A CURVE CUT INTO THE STRINGER WHERE THE SEAT SLATS ARE ATTACHED.

roll line. Or, cut out cardboard templates for guides, or use plastic curved rulers from an art supply store. It doesn't matter what shape your line is, ultimately, because you are going to use the first stringer as the master to cut others. As long as the stringers match each other, you can (within reason and limits of comfort) have the line do anything you want.

Rolling seats do present a problem with slat width. A $5/4$ x 4 slat may be too wide, given the radius of your curve. The slat might "bridge" the radius and defeat the curve by flattening it. The seat slats would work better if they were thinner, say $5/4$ x 3s or $5/4$ x 2s (see above, right).

Once you have your rolling line drawn and cut, lay in a couple of seat slats to see how they sit in the curve. Then try thinner slats. You can make the slats thinner by running them through a table saw. Since we are using one screw in each slat, and we are predrilling, you run the risk of splitting only the narrowest of slats.

■A FANCY FRONT BRACE

You may want to cut along the bottom of your front brace to add a little flair to the design. So long as you cut less than a third out of the brace, you won't hurt its structural ability to hold weight. As you'll see, cutting a third gives you a good-sized area to work in. The drawings below show design suggestions but feel free

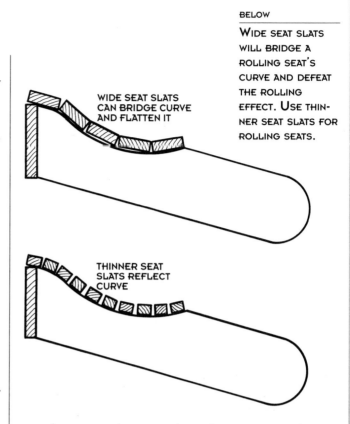

WIDE SEAT SLATS CAN BRIDGE CURVE AND FLATTEN IT

THINNER SEAT SLATS REFLECT CURVE

BELOW

WIDE SEAT SLATS WILL BRIDGE A ROLLING SEAT'S CURVE AND DEFEAT THE ROLLING EFFECT. USE THINNER SEAT SLATS FOR ROLLING SEATS.

to make up any design you wish. The design can be cut with a saber saw, just like the other curved cuts mentioned elsewhere in this book. To draw these curves, use the same pencil-on-a-string technique explained earlier. As I mentioned earlier, some

graphic-arts stores have curved rulers, or guides, with which you can draw some interesting designs. Don't overlook design tools available in your own home—the bottom of an oval office trash can, for example, can serve as a template for some great curves.

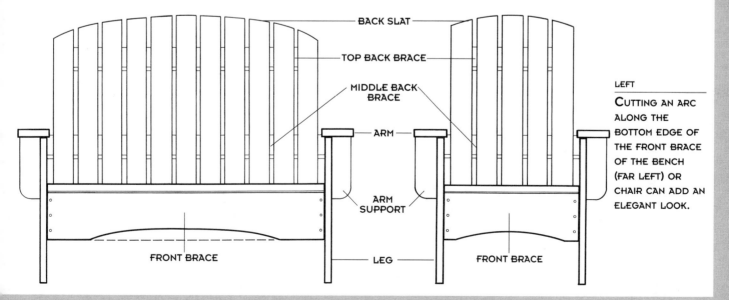

BACK SLAT

TOP BACK BRACE

MIDDLE BACK BRACE

ARM

ARM SUPPORT

FRONT BRACE

LEG

FRONT BRACE

LEFT

CUTTING AN ARC ALONG THE BOTTOM EDGE OF THE FRONT BRACE OF THE BENCH (FAR LEFT) OR CHAIR CAN ADD AN ELEGANT LOOK.

ASSEMBLING THE ADIRONDACK CHAIR

4

BACK SLATS

TOP BACK BRACE

MIDDLE BACK BRACE

SEAT SLATS

STRINGER

FRONT BRACE

RIGHT

THIS ADIRONDACK
CHAIR IS MADE
FROM COMMON
LUMBER STOCK.
STRINGERS AND
LOWER BACK BRACE
ARE $^5/_4$ x **8**; ARMS
ARE $^5/_4$ x **6**, AND
BACK AND SEAT
SLATS ARE $^5/_4$ x **4**.

LOWER BACK BRACE

AFTER YOU'VE CUT THE NECESSARY PIECES OF WOOD FROM THE CUT
list into the lengths marked on the cutting diagram and then
sanded them, it's time to assemble the chair.

Start by loading a variable-speed drill with a #8 counter-
sink/predrill bit. Whenever we insert a screw, it will go into a predilled
hole created by this countersink. The predrilled hole helps stop the
wood from splitting, and the countersink allows the head of the screw
to sit below the surface of the board. (Later, we'll fill this countersink
hole with a plug of the same kind of wood as the chair itself.)

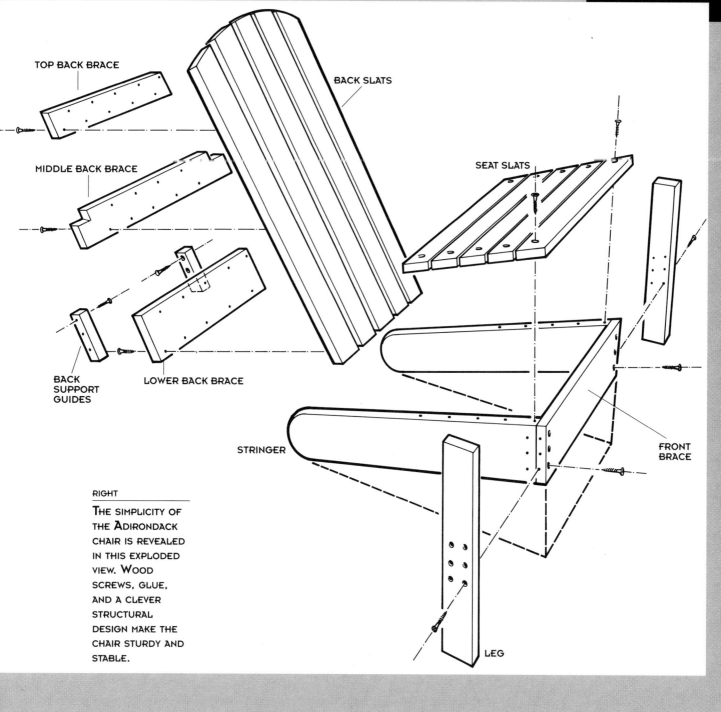

TOP BACK BRACE

BACK SLATS

MIDDLE BACK BRACE

SEAT SLATS

BACK
SUPPORT
GUIDES

LOWER BACK BRACE

STRINGER

FRONT
BRACE

LEG

RIGHT

THE SIMPLICITY OF
THE ADIRONDACK
CHAIR IS REVEALED
IN THIS EXPLODED
VIEW. WOOD
SCREWS, GLUE,
AND A CLEVER
STRUCTURAL
DESIGN MAKE THE
CHAIR STURDY AND
STABLE.

You'll find it convenient to have two drills: one set up with the countersink/predrill bit, and one set up with a Phillips bit (the cross-shaped drive bit) for driving screws. That way you can drill a bunch of holes and then, without stopping to change bits, drive screws. Since the countersink bit penetrates both boards (drill with boards in place whenever possible), you risk moving the under board and losing the predrill hole alignment if you're messing around changing from drill bit to drive bit.

O.K., on to assembling the chair.

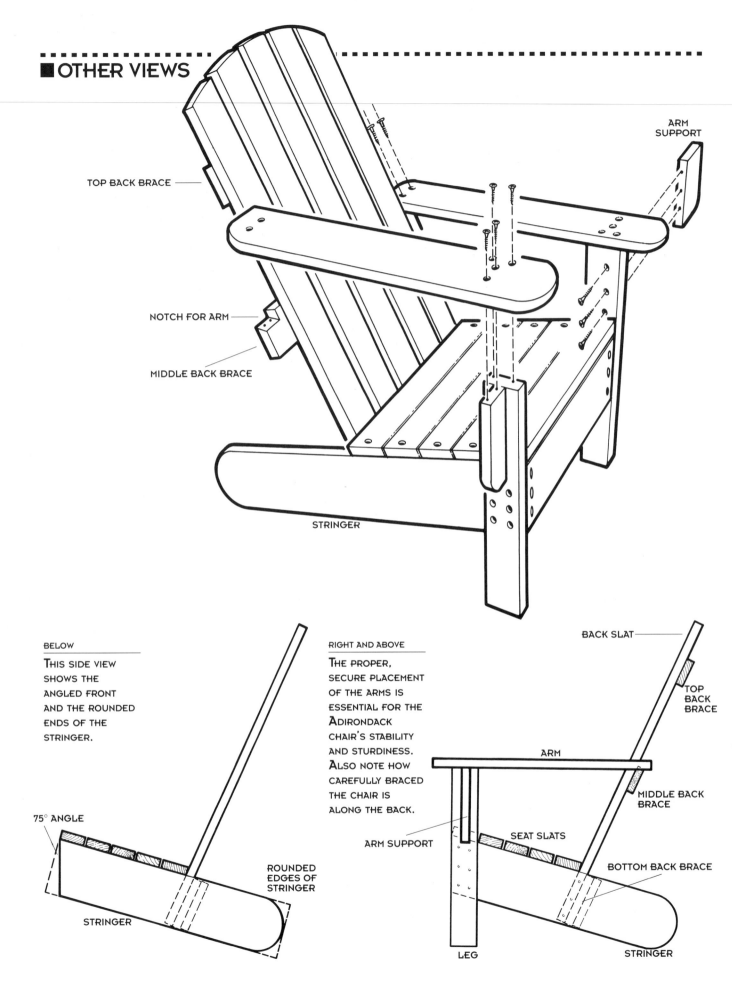

TOP BACK BRACE

ARM SUPPORT

NOTCH FOR ARM

MIDDLE BACK BRACE

STRINGER

BELOW

THIS SIDE VIEW SHOWS THE ANGLED FRONT AND THE ROUNDED ENDS OF THE STRINGER.

75° ANGLE

STRINGER

ROUNDED EDGES OF STRINGER

RIGHT AND ABOVE

THE PROPER, SECURE PLACEMENT OF THE ARMS IS ESSENTIAL FOR THE ADIRONDACK CHAIR'S STABILITY AND STURDINESS. ALSO NOTE HOW CAREFULLY BRACED THE CHAIR IS ALONG THE BACK.

ARM SUPPORT

ARM

SEAT SLATS

LEG

BACK SLAT

TOP BACK BRACE

MIDDLE BACK BRACE

BOTTOM BACK BRACE

STRINGER

LUMBER LIST

- ○ (1) 10 foot $^5/_4$ x 8
- ○ (4) 10 foot $^5/_4$ x 4
- ○ (1) 6 foot $^5/_4$ x 6

BELOW

USE THIS CUTTING DIAGRAM AND LUMBER LIST WHEN PURCHASING LUMBER AND CUTTING CHAIR PARTS.

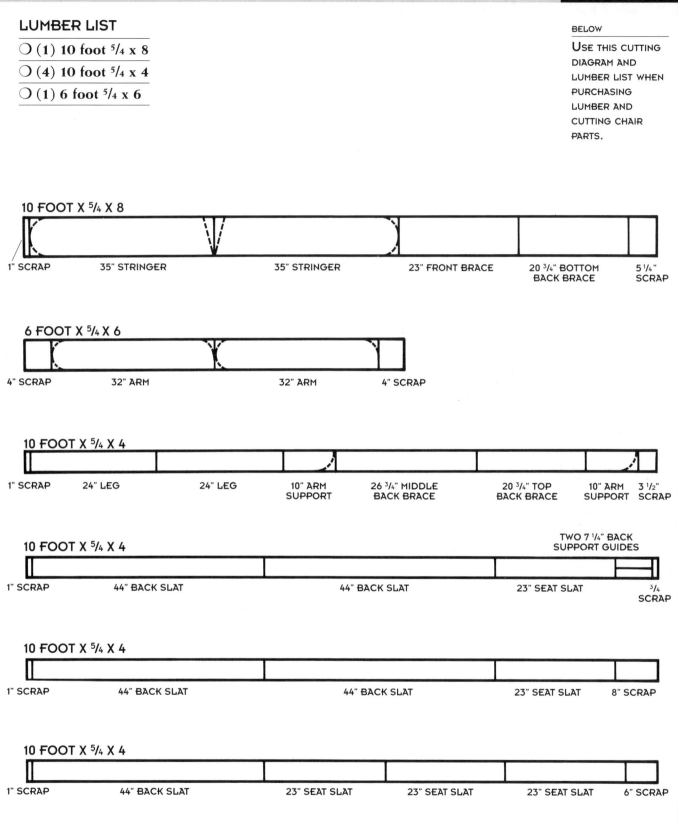

10 FOOT X $^5/_4$ X 8

| 1" SCRAP | 35" STRINGER | 35" STRINGER | 23" FRONT BRACE | 20 $^3/_4$" BOTTOM BACK BRACE | 5 $^1/_4$" SCRAP |

6 FOOT X $^5/_4$ X 6

| 4" SCRAP | 32" ARM | 32" ARM | 4" SCRAP |

10 FOOT X $^5/_4$ X 4

| 1" SCRAP | 24" LEG | 24" LEG | 10" ARM SUPPORT | 26 $^3/_4$" MIDDLE BACK BRACE | 20 $^3/_4$" TOP BACK BRACE | 10" ARM SUPPORT | 3 $^1/_2$" SCRAP |

10 FOOT X $^5/_4$ X 4

TWO 7 $^1/_4$" BACK SUPPORT GUIDES

| 1" SCRAP | 44" BACK SLAT | 44" BACK SLAT | 23" SEAT SLAT | $^3/_4$ SCRAP |

10 FOOT X $^5/_4$ X 4

| 1" SCRAP | 44" BACK SLAT | 44" BACK SLAT | 23" SEAT SLAT | 8" SCRAP |

10 FOOT X $^5/_4$ X 4

| 1" SCRAP | 44" BACK SLAT | 23" SEAT SLAT | 23" SEAT SLAT | 23" SEAT SLAT | 6" SCRAP |

ASSEMBLING THE BACK

■ THE BOTTOM BACK BRACE

START BY LAYING THE FIVE BACK SLATS NEXT TO each other on the worktable. (Whatever side of the boards faces down will ultimately rest against your back when you sit in the chair, so face knots up toward you now.) Then lay your 20 3/4-inch bottom back brace (the 5/4 x 8-inch board—the widest of the three back braces) on top of the five back slats, at one end. Place one back slat at each end of the brace (we'll set the spacing between the inner slats in a moment), and square them to the back brace's edges. We will eventually drive screws down through the bottom back brace into all the back slats, but we are only doing the outside ones first.

For each end slat, we'll predrill for two screws, making sure to align the holes on a diagonal with each other. That way, the screws won't split the wood by being in the same grain line. To make the screw holes symmetrically diagonal, drive them 1 inch in from each edge. Never drive the screws too close to the edge, certainly not closer than 1/2 inch.

Once you have the countersink holes drilled for each of the two end slats, drive

1 BELOW

USE A SQUARE TO ENSURE THAT YOUR BOTTOM BACK BRACE IS SQUARE TO THE SLATS. DOUBLE-CHECK THE SLATS' POSITION BEFORE SCREWING THEM IN PLACE.

two #8 1 ½-inch wood screws so the heads sit snug at the bottom of the countersink hole.

Now position the remaining three back slats and space them evenly to take up the distance between the two end slats you've just installed. The distance between back slats should be the same. Given a bottom back brace length of 20 ¾ inches, the distance between back slats should be just over ⅝ inches (a "fat" ⅝). But your boards may vary. Establish a standard distance between the slats, check it with your tape measure and eye, and—when you're happy with how things look—screw down the remaining slats. To maintain a consistent distance between slats, you may want to cut a couple ⅝-inch blocks to use as spacers while you're screwing the slats down.

When screwing the remaining back slats down, lay out your screw holes so they repeat the layout of screws on the end slats. That will give the screw holes a nice symmetry.

Do not pick up this assembly! It is not strong enough to move. Leave everything right where it is and go to the next step.

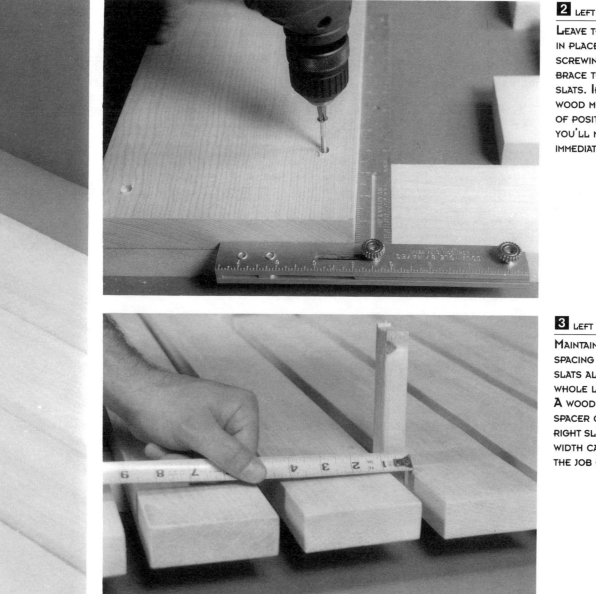

2 LEFT
LEAVE THE SQUARE IN PLACE WHEN SCREWING THE BRACE TO THE SLATS. IF THE WOOD MOVES OUT OF POSITION, YOU'LL NOTICE IMMEDIATELY.

3 LEFT
MAINTAIN THE SAME SPACING BETWEEN SLATS ALONG THEIR WHOLE LENGTH. A WOOD-BLOCK SPACER CUT TO THE RIGHT SLAT-SPACE WIDTH CAN MAKE THE JOB EASIER.

1 ABOVE

POSITION THE TOP BACK BRACE WITH A TAPE MEASURE AND SQUARE WORKING IN TANDEM.

2 ABOVE

LEAVE THE SQUARE IN PLACE WHEN DRIVING SCREWS HOME. THAT WAY, BOARD MOVEMENT WILL BE IMMEDIATELY EVIDENT.

POSITION THE 20 3/4-INCH TOP BACK BRACE 8 inches down from the top of the back slats. Use a square to position it. Then, kneeling on it, predrill and screw into place *only the outside slats* so they are flush to the outside of the top back brace. (When predrilling, make the same diagonal pattern that you made along the bottom brace.)

Now recheck the 5/8-inch spacing between all the slats (use your block spacers, if you have them, before screwing the inner ones in place). It should match the slat spacing along the bottom back brace. Look good? Drill and screw through the top back brace to the remaining slats beneath it, maintaining the same diagonal screw pattern you established earlier.

3 LEFT

ESTABLISH AND MAINTAIN A STANDARD DIAGONAL PATTERN FOR THE SCREWS ON ALL THREE BACK BRACES.

LEFT

PROPER PLACE-
MENT OF THE
MIDDLE BACK
BRACE IS CRUCIAL
FOR MAINTAINING
LEVEL ARMS. NOTE
THE SQUARE AT THE
TOP OF THE PHOTO.
WHEN POSITIONING
BOARDS, ALWAYS
USE A SQUARE.

THE PLACEMENT OF THE MIDDLE BACK BRACE IS crucial because its height will determine the height of the back of the arms. Since our arms will be level (parallel with the ground) place the bottom edge of the middle brace 18 5/8 inches up from the bottom of the slats. This height accounts for notches we'll later cut out of the brace to rest the arms in. (If you want your arms to slope back a bit and you have cut the 5-degree bevels in the front legs and arm supports, place the bottom of the middle brace 16 1/4 inches from the bottom of the back slats.)

You'll notice that the middle back brace is longer than the slats are wide. Place the middle back brace so that approximately 3 inches protrude from either side of the back slats (be sure both sides have the same amount of brace protruding, even if it isn't exactly 3 inches). Before you drill and screw this brace into place, make sure it is square to the bottom and top braces, and square to the slats. After you've double-checked, drill and screw the brace into place. Be sure to stagger your screws diagonally so that they aren't screwed into the same grain and so they reflect the pattern you established on the other two braces.

Except for cutting out decorative curves across the top of the slats and notching the middle brace, the back of the chair is done. Put it aside.

ASSEMBLING THE STRINGER
■ INSTALLING THE FRONT BRACE

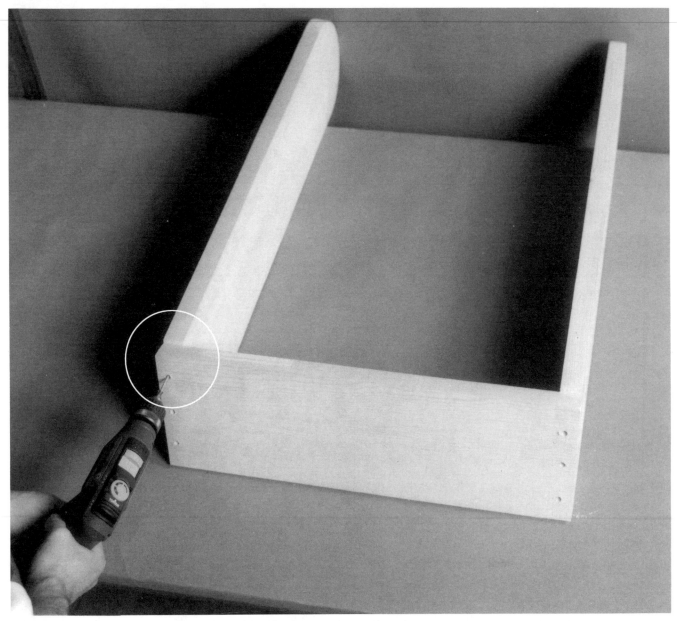

ABOVE

SECURELY SCREW THE FRONT BRACE TO THE STRINGER WITH THREE SCREWS—EVENLY SPACED—ON EITHER END OF THE BRACE.

WE'VE ALREADY CUT THE FRONT END OF EACH stringer with a 75-degree angle (we cut half circles at the back ends). Be sure you attach your front brace to the angled front part of both stringers.

Predrill three holes 1/2 inch in from each end of the front brace: one in the center (about 3 5/8 inches in from either edge), and the others 1 5/8 inches in from the top and bottom edges. Hold the brace up to the front of the angled end of the stringer and drive your screws home. Be sure you rest your brace against the stringer so the top of the brace is flush with what will be the top of the stringer.

You will see that the face of the stringer's end grain is wider than the front brace is tall. You may want to trim or taper the stringer so it matches the front brace's width (see circle in photo). But it's not necessary.

THE FRONT LEG IS SECURED WITH SIX SCREWS: THREE DRIVEN INTO THE FRONT BRACE AND THREE INTO THE SIDE OF THE STRINGER.

IT WILL BE EASIEST TO SET THE STRINGER ASSEMBLY on its side to screw on the legs, but since the back end (the curved end) of the stringers aren't secured, the stringer will flop around if you do this. To avoid this problem, insert a temporary spacer between the stringer's curved end. That way you don't risk ripping out the front-brace screws when setting the piece on its side.

On one of the chair's 24-inch front-leg boards, make a mark at 15 inches. Lay the leg so that the front of it is flush with the front of the front brace.

The top of the front brace should line up with the 15-inch mark on the leg. In other words, when your chair is finished and sitting upright, the top of your front brace will sit 15 inches above the ground.

Drill and screw in six screws: three through the leg into the end grain of the front brace and three through the leg into the side of the stringers. As always, stagger these screws slightly to defeat splitting.

Flip the stringer assembly over and repeat the procedure. (You will find you'll have to block the stringer so it sits level, since the leg you just installed will elevate it on one end.)

Once both legs are installed, set the stringer upright on its legs. It's time to mark where and at what angle the back will sit.

MARKING FOR THE BACK PLACEMENT

WE KNOW AT WHAT ANGLE THE CHAIR'S back will tilt. It's 100 degrees. But where do we mark the guidelines for the back? Where exactly will the back sit along the stringer's top edge?

Wherever it sits, it must leave enough room for five seat slats. The seat slats are 3 ½ inches wide—that's 17 ½ total inches. Add four between-slat spaces of, say, ⅛ inch for a ½ inch total, and we find the seat will occupy 18 inches total along the stringer.

So, the face of the chair's back (the part you will actually rest your back against) must sit 18 inches back from where the seat slats start. Since the first seat slat will be flush with the front of the front brace, measure 18 inches back from there. Make marks on both stringers.

Put your protractor on the inside of the stringers, set it at 100 degrees, and draw a line along this 100-degree edge.

You may want to increase or decrease the angle of the back. Some people like a 90-degree angle between the back and the seat, some people want something more reclining, say, 120 degrees. It's up to you. But if you increase or decrease this angle, it will affect the height of the middle back brace, which will in turn affect the slope of the arms. If you monkey around with the angle of the back, be sure to account for it when placing the middle brace and when cutting the bevels on the front legs and the arms supports.

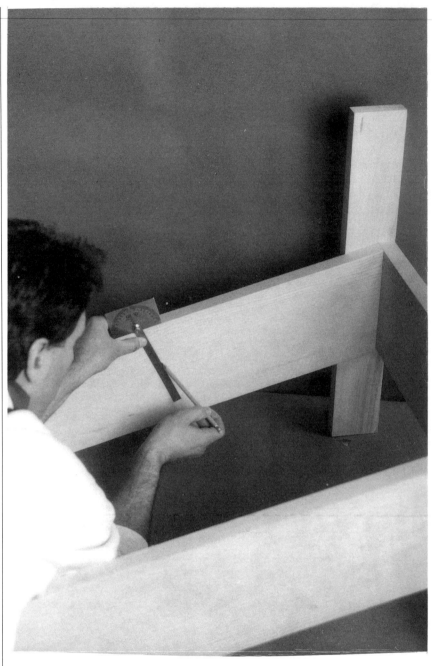

ABOVE

USE A PROTRAC-TOR TO MARK THE ANGLE FOR BACK PLACEMENT, LEAVING A FULL 18 INCHES ALONG THE STRINGERS FOR SEAT SLATS.

1 LEFT

USING THE PLACEMENT LINES YOU DREW WITH YOUR PROTRACTOR AS A GUIDE, INSTALL THE BACK. ALIGN THE FRONT EDGE OF THE BACK SLATS WITH THE LINE.

SINCE WE HAVE THE BACK ASSEMBLED, WE NEED only install it between the stringers. We just drew the guidelines for the 100-degree angle, so we know where to position the back between the stringers. But positioning the back is a two-person job. You need a person to hold it in place while you screw through the stringers into the bottom back brace (don't screw into the slats). Predrill these screw holes in the stringers so they are all lined up for when the back is properly positioned.

Insert the assembled back between the stringers and line up the front of the slats to the 100-degree guidelines. Also, position the bottom of the back slats so they are flush with the underside edge of the stringer. With an assistant holding the back in place, drill and screw three screws for each side. Screw from the outside of the stringer into the bottom back brace, (not the slats). Once the screws are driven in, your assistant can let go of the back.

We have to add some support to the back

in the form of back support blocks; otherwise, the six screws would be bearing most of the weight of someone sitting in the bench. Position the two precut 2 x 5/4 back support guides snug up against the bottom back brace. Working from the inside (between the stringers), drill and screw these blocks into place by screwing sideways into the stringer. Use three screws in each block.

2 ABOVE

ONCE THE BACK IS IN PLACE, SCREW A SUPPORT BLOCK BEHIND IT AND INTO EACH STRINGER, USING THREE SCREWS.

Installing the Arms

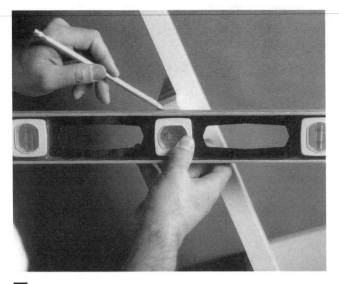

1 ABOVE

To notch out a pad or "seat" where the back end of the arm will be screwed into place, start by using a level to draw the seat line.

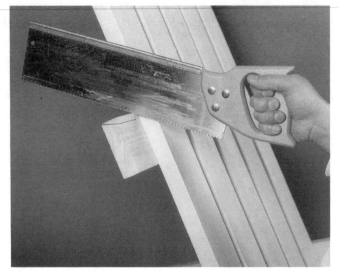

2 ABOVE

Using a handsaw, cut out the small section of wood you have marked.

If you've done all your measurements and installation right, once you make a ¾-inch notch in the middle back brace, you should be able to lay the chair's arms on and have them sit level. The reason we are making the notch is to provide a level surface area (a "seat") into which the arms can be screwed. If we didn't make the notch, the back ends of the arms would be sitting on the angled edge of the middle back brace—an unsound connection that would soon break apart.

How do you make this notch? How wide and deep should it be? Well, you want it to be ¾ inches deep, so there is plenty of surface area for securing the arm. Measure down ¾ inches from the topmost part of the middle back brace and make a mark. Then hold your level up to this mark and draw a level line. This is your depth line.

To determine the notch's width, lay one of the chair arms in place over the back brace. Let it hang ½ inch over the inside of the front leg and 4 inches over the front. The arm will naturally rest on the middle back brace where it is supposed to sit, but don't put the inside edge of the arm flush with the back slats. There should be roughly a ¾-inch space between them. Lay the arm in place and mark on the middle brace where the arm will sit.

Once you have the depth and width marked, you can trace with a pencil how much wood to cut out. Then, with your handsaw, make careful cuts to remove this wood.

When you've finished the cut, use a sharp, 1-inch chisel to chip away the excess wood until the notch is accurately cut and shaved smooth.

Lay the arm in place and drill and screw two screws down into the front leg. Then drill and screw two screws into the notch. These screws should be drilled at an angle into the notches, so the screws are driven into the center of the back brace.

The chair arm should feel pretty secure, but there is one more thing to do: install the arm supports.

3 ABOVE

NEXT, USE A SHARP
CHISEL TO MAKE
THE CUT SMOOTH
AND LEVEL.

4 ABOVE

ANGLE YOUR
SCREWS WHEN
SCREWING THE
BACK END OF THE
ARM IN PLACE.

5 RIGHT

SECURE THE FRONT
OF THE ARM BY
DRIVING TWO
SCREWS THROUGH
IT AND INTO THE
TOP OF THE LEG.

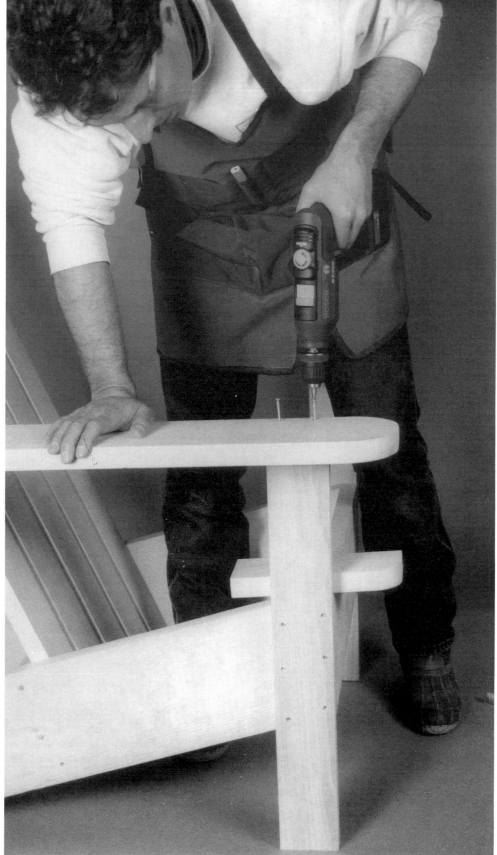

■ INSTALLING THE ARM SUPPORTS

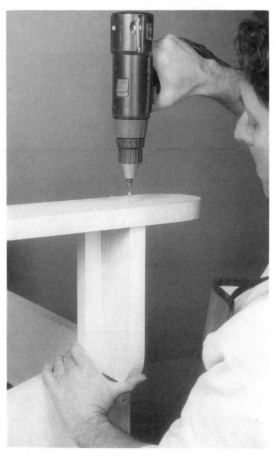

1 ABOVE

FIRST, SECURE THE ARM SUPPORT FROM THE SIDE WITH THREE SCREWS DRIVEN FROM THE INSIDE OF THE LEG.

POSITION AN ARM SUPPORT ON THE OUTSIDE OF a front leg so it is centered and snug up under the arm. It should fit in there square. (If not, the cut on the top of your leg is not square, and your arm is angled, not flat—or your middle back brace is not positioned properly.)

With this arm support firmly in place, drill and screw from the inside of the front leg into the arm support with three screws.

Be sure to position the screws so they are centered and equidistant from each other and equidistant from the ends of the arm support.

Then, from above, drill and screw two more screws through your arm and into the arm support.

In the end, there will be five screws in the arm support: two screws driven in from above, through the arm, and into the support; and three screws driven from the side, through the front leg and into the support.

That's a lot of screws to drive into such a small piece of wood. To defeat splitting, do a thorough job of predrilling, and make sure all the screws are centered. If the arm support splits open, it's no big deal. You can make another rather quickly from some scrap ends. Of course, the best thing to do is start with a quality piece of wood and carefully drive the screws.

Once you've attached the arm supports, your work is done on this part of the chair.

2 LEFT

NOW DRIVE TWO SCREWS THROUGH THE ARM AND INTO THE TOP OF THE ARM SUPPORT.

INSTALLING THE SEAT SLATS

YOU'RE GETTING CLOSE NOW. LET'S INSTALL THE seat slats and finish this project!

Lay out all five seat slats and space them on the stringer so they take up the seat space evenly. You should leave about ⅛ inch between them. But there are lots of variables here and you may end up leaving more space, depending on where the chair's back sits. Once you have the seat slats laid out, (yes, lay out all of them before screwing any down) drill and screw them into place. Use just one screw for each end of each seat slat.

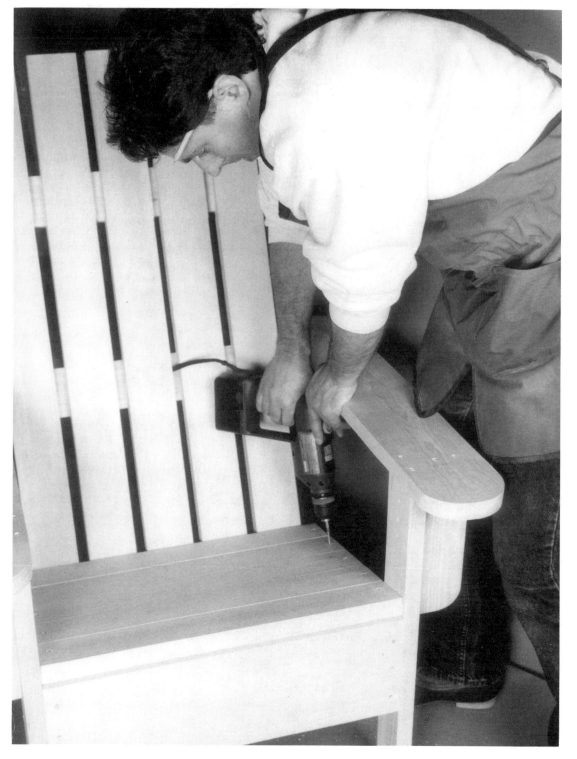

1 LEFT
USE JUST ONE SCREW AT THE END OF EACH SEAT SLAT, SCREWING DOWN INTO THE STRINGER.

PLUGGING THE SCREW HOLES

If you've drilled your countersinks to the right depth, you should be able to take some 5/16-inch plugs (of whatever wood you are using: use pine plugs if your chair's wood is pine) dab them in some glue or epoxy, and tap one into each of the screw holes.

Be careful when applying the glue so that globs of it don't over-spill onto the wood face. Sure you can sand this off, but the wood absorbs some of the glue, and when you finish the chair, these areas will take the finish differently.

When tapped into place, the plugs will actually sit just above the surface of the wood. After the glue has dried, the easiest thing to do is to belt sand these plugs flush. Or you can take a razor-sharp chisel and cut the top of the plugs flush with the chair's wood surfaces.

1 LEFT

TAP EPOXY-COATED WOOD PLUGS INTO THE COUNTERSINK HOLES. MIX THE EPOXY ON THE TOP OF A CAN OR OTHER CLEAN SURFACE.

2 LEFT

ONCE THE GLUE IS COMPLETELY DRY, USE A CHISEL TO SHAVE THE EXCESS WOOD FROM THE WOOD PLUG.

3 LEFT

FINISH BY BELT-SANDING OR PALM-SANDING THE PLUGS, BEING CAREFUL NOT TO GOUGE THE WOOD.

SAND, SEAL, AND SIT

THE NEXT THING TO DO IS SAND THE HECK OUT of the finished product with #220 sandpaper. Sand off all the pencil marks and wherever the wood's gotten dirty from handling. Then, flip ahead to chapter 10 for tips on choosing sealer, urethane, or paint to finish the chair.

ASSEMBLING
THE
ADIRONDACK
BENCH

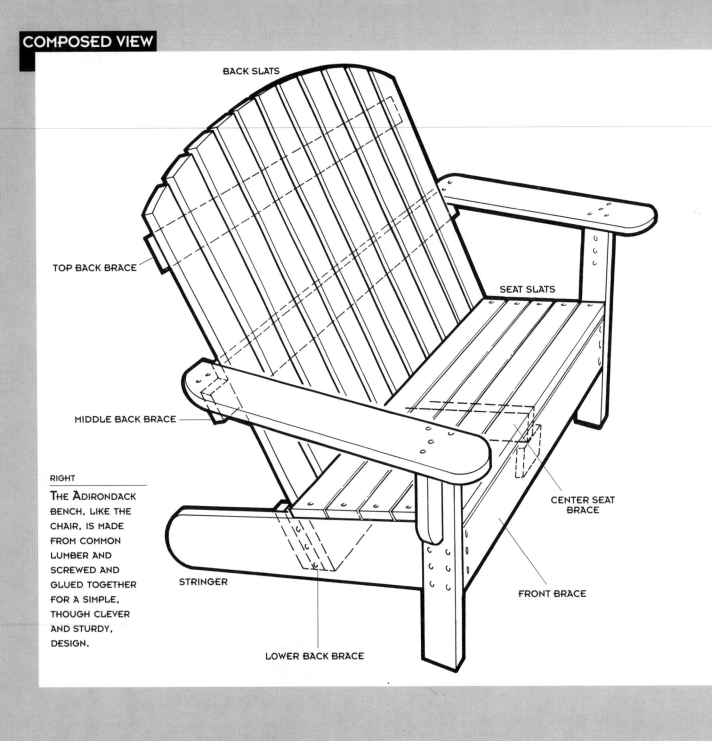

BACK SLATS

TOP BACK BRACE

SEAT SLATS

MIDDLE BACK BRACE

RIGHT

THE ADIRONDACK
BENCH, LIKE THE
CHAIR, IS MADE
FROM COMMON
LUMBER AND
SCREWED AND
GLUED TOGETHER
FOR A SIMPLE,
THOUGH CLEVER
AND STURDY,
DESIGN.

CENTER SEAT
BRACE

STRINGER

FRONT BRACE

LOWER BACK BRACE

I F YOU'RE BUILDING THE ADIRONDACK BENCH AFTER YOU'VE BUILT THE Adirondack chair, you'll find that the assembly methods (and many components) are the same. In fact, if you want to build both the chair and the bench, study the cutting diagrams ahead of time, because you can probably "gang-cut" many of the pieces during one session.

As you'll see, the Adirondack bench is really a wider version of the Adirondack chair from the previous chapter. The arms, stringers, and vertical front legs are all the same. Only the length of the seat slats, the length of the front and back braces, and the number of back slats are different.

If you didn't build the Adirondack chair, and you're starting in with the bench, this chapter lays out, step by step, everything you need to know.

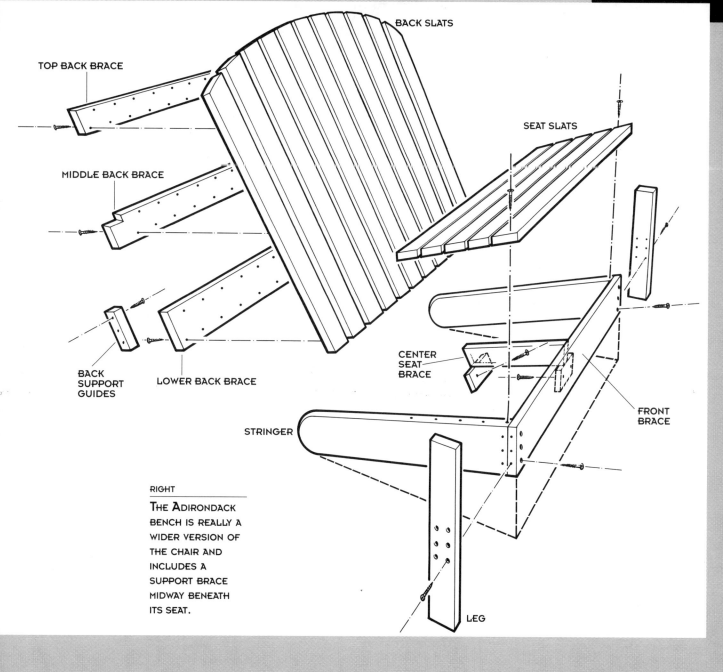

TOP BACK BRACE

BACK SLATS

MIDDLE BACK BRACE

SEAT SLATS

BACK SUPPORT GUIDES

LOWER BACK BRACE

CENTER SEAT BRACE

FRONT BRACE

STRINGER

RIGHT

THE ADIRONDACK BENCH IS REALLY A WIDER VERSION OF THE CHAIR AND INCLUDES A SUPPORT BRACE MIDWAY BENEATH ITS SEAT.

LEG

After you've cut and sanded all the pieces of wood from the cut list into the lengths marked on the cutting diagram, you're ready to assemble the bench. (Be sure to cut the curves on the arms and stringers ahead of time. For a brushup on how to do that, take a look at "Marking and Cutting Curves," page 31.)

Oh, and here's a time-saving hint on tools before we start: As with any of the projects in this book, it's very convenient to use two variable-speed drills. One should be loaded with a #8 countersink/predrill bit, the other with a Phillips drive bit (the cross-shaped drive bit). Of course one drill will do fine. You'll just find yourself changing drill bits perhaps more times than you wish.

■ OTHER VIEWS

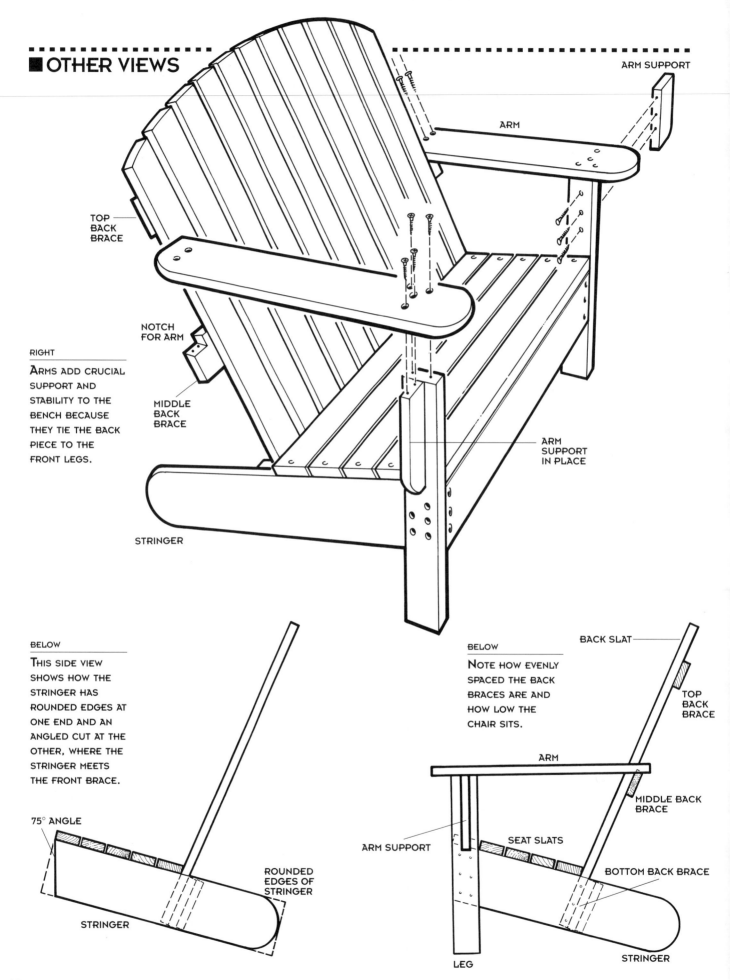

ARM SUPPORT

ARM

TOP BACK BRACE

NOTCH FOR ARM

RIGHT

ARMS ADD CRUCIAL SUPPORT AND STABILITY TO THE BENCH BECAUSE THEY TIE THE BACK PIECE TO THE FRONT LEGS.

MIDDLE BACK BRACE

ARM SUPPORT IN PLACE

STRINGER

BELOW

THIS SIDE VIEW SHOWS HOW THE STRINGER HAS ROUNDED EDGES AT ONE END AND AN ANGLED CUT AT THE OTHER, WHERE THE STRINGER MEETS THE FRONT BRACE.

75° ANGLE

ROUNDED EDGES OF STRINGER

STRINGER

BELOW

NOTE HOW EVENLY SPACED THE BACK BRACES ARE AND HOW LOW THE CHAIR SITS.

BACK SLAT

TOP BACK BRACE

ARM

MIDDLE BACK BRACE

ARM SUPPORT

SEAT SLATS

BOTTOM BACK BRACE

LEG

STRINGER

CUTTING GUIDE

BELOW

Use this diagram and lumber list when shopping for lumber and cutting the pieces for your bench.

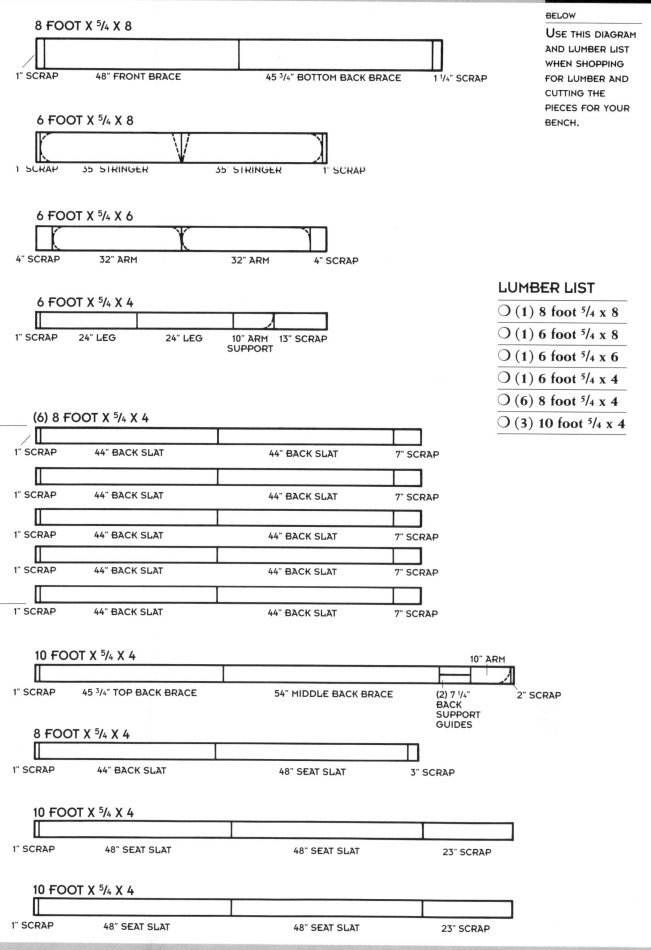

8 FOOT X ⁵/₄ X 8

1" SCRAP | 48" FRONT BRACE | 45 ¾" BOTTOM BACK BRACE | 1 ¼" SCRAP

6 FOOT X ⁵/₄ X 8

1" SCRAP | 35" STRINGER | 35" STRINGER | 1" SCRAP

6 FOOT X ⁵/₄ X 6

4" SCRAP | 32" ARM | 32" ARM | 4" SCRAP

6 FOOT X ⁵/₄ X 4

1" SCRAP | 24" LEG | 24" LEG | 10" ARM SUPPORT | 13" SCRAP

(6) 8 FOOT X ⁵/₄ X 4

1" SCRAP | 44" BACK SLAT | 44" BACK SLAT | 7" SCRAP

1" SCRAP | 44" BACK SLAT | 44" BACK SLAT | 7" SCRAP

1" SCRAP | 44" BACK SLAT | 44" BACK SLAT | 7" SCRAP

1" SCRAP | 44" BACK SLAT | 44" BACK SLAT | 7" SCRAP

1" SCRAP | 44" BACK SLAT | 44" BACK SLAT | 7" SCRAP

10 FOOT X ⁵/₄ X 4

10" ARM

1" SCRAP | 45 ¾" TOP BACK BRACE | 54" MIDDLE BACK BRACE | (2) 7 ¼" BACK SUPPORT GUIDES | 2" SCRAP

8 FOOT X ⁵/₄ X 4

1" SCRAP | 44" BACK SLAT | 48" SEAT SLAT | 3" SCRAP

10 FOOT X ⁵/₄ X 4

1" SCRAP | 48" SEAT SLAT | 48" SEAT SLAT | 23" SCRAP

10 FOOT X ⁵/₄ X 4

1" SCRAP | 48" SEAT SLAT | 48" SEAT SLAT | 23" SCRAP

LUMBER LIST

- ○ (1) 8 foot ⁵/₄ x 8
- ○ (1) 6 foot ⁵/₄ x 8
- ○ (1) 6 foot ⁵/₄ x 6
- ○ (1) 6 foot ⁵/₄ x 4
- ○ (6) 8 foot ⁵/₄ x 4
- ○ (3) 10 foot ⁵/₄ x 4

Assembling the Back

■ THE BOTTOM BACK BRACE

BEFORE ASSEMBLING THE BENCH'S BACK, HAVE A helper on hand. The Adirondack bench's back will be large, unwieldy, and somewhat heavy. Once it is assembled, it will surely take two people to install: at least one to hold it and one to screw it in place. Even if you were able to install the Adirondack chair's back by your-self, think twice before trying it on the bench. Have a friend drop over for this part of the job. (While there, why not get your friend to do some sanding! Say things like, "You know I never realized how *really fun* sanding is. Here, give it a try." The old Tom-Sawyer-and-the-fence trick still works—sometimes.)

1 ABOVE

SCREW THROUGH THE LOWER BACK BRACE AND INTO THE BACK SLATS. ESTABLISH A DIAGONAL PATTERN FOR SCREW PLACEMENT AND MAINTAIN THAT PATTERN ON ALL THE BACK BRACES.

LAY THE ELEVEN BACK SLATS NEXT TO EACH OTHER on the worktable. Then lay your 45 3/4-inch bottom back brace (the 5/4 x 8 board—the widest back brace) on top of the eleven back slats. Place one back slat at each end of the bottom brace (we'll set the spacing between the inner slats in a minute), and square them to the bottom back brace's edges.

For each end slat, countersink/predrill two holes, but don't align your screws with the center of the back slat. Instead, drive the screws in a diagonal pattern. That way, the screws won't split the wood by being in the same grain line. Also, never drive a screw closer than 1 inch to any edge of the brace.

For each end slat, drive two #8 1 1/2 inch flathead wood screws firmly, so the heads sit snug at the bottom of the countersink holes.

Now position the remaining nine back slats and space them evenly to take up the

distance between the two end back slats you've just installed. The distance between all the back slats should be the same. Given a bottom back brace width of 45 3/4, the distance between each back slat should be just under 3/4 inches (or a "fat" 5/8). To maintain consistent spacing, you may want to cut two 3/4-inch spacer blocks to use between the back slats.

Your slats may vary in width. So, install your end back slats, establish a standard distance between the remaining slats, check the distance with your tape measure and eye, and—when everything looks right—screw down the rest of the back slats.

Do not lift this back assembly! It is not strong enough to move. Leave everything right where it is and go on to the next step.

2 ABOVE

A WOOD-BLOCK SPACER CUT TO THE PROPER WIDTH CAN BE USED AS A GUIDE WHEN SCREWING BACK SLATS IN PLACE.

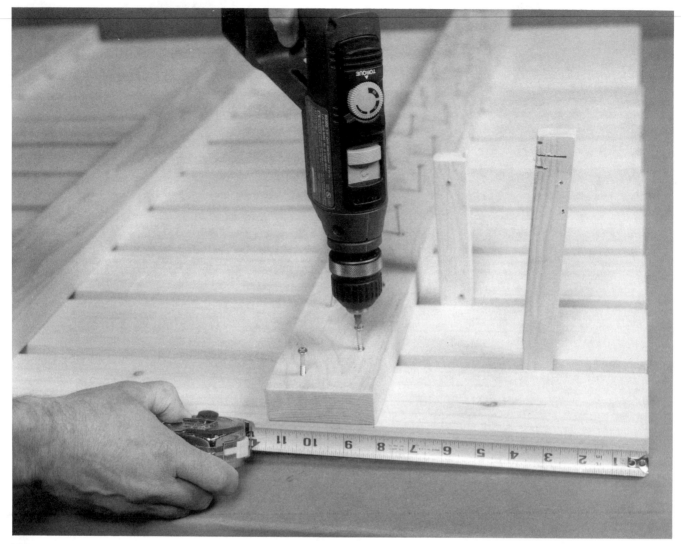

POSITION THE TOP BACK BRACE 8 INCHES DOWN FROM THE TOP OF THE BACK SLATS. NOTE HOW THE DIAGONAL SCREW PATTERN IS THE SAME AS THE PATTERN ESTABLISHED ON THE OTHER TWO BACK BRACES.

POSITION THE 45 3/4-INCH TOP BACK BRACE 8 inches down from the top of the back slats. Use a square to position it. Then, kneeling on it, predrill and screw in place *just the end slats* so you can recheck the spacing distance between the inner slats before screwing them in place.

With the end slats securely screwed in place, recheck the 3/4-inch spacing between all the slats. (It should match the slat spacing from the bottom.) Once the spacing looks good, drill and screw through the top back brace to the remaining slats beneath it. Here, as elsewhere, use two #8 1 1/2-inch wood screws for each slat. Drive the screws in a diagonal pattern and position them a minimum of 1 inch from each edge.

PROPER PLACEMENT OF THIS MIDDLE BACK BRACE is crucial because its height will determine the height of the back of the arms. We want our arms to be level (parallel with the ground), so place the bottom edge of the middle brace 18 ⅝ inches up from the bottom of the slats. This measurement takes into account two ¾-inch notches we'll cut out of the middle back brace to rest the arms in. (If you want your arms to slope back a bit and you have cut the 5-degree bevels in the front legs and arm supports, place the bottom edge of the middle brace 16 ¼ inches from the bottom of the back slats.)

Position the middle back brace so an equal number of inches of its length protrude from either side of the back slats. Since the back slats are 45 ¾ inches wide and the middle brace is 52 inches long, you should have just over 3 inches (3 ⅛ inches, actually) protruding from either side.

Before you drill and screw this brace into place, use a square to make sure the brace is square to the bottom and top braces, and square to the slats.

After you've double-checked all your measurements, drill and screw the brace into place. Be sure to stagger your screws in a diagonal pattern so the screws aren't screwed into the same center grain line and so they reflect the pattern you've established on the other braces.

We have some more work to do on the bench back later, but for now put it aside.

ABOVE

THE MIDDLE BACK BRACE SHOULD PROTRUDE 3 INCHES BEYOND THE OUTERMOST BACK SLATS. WHEN THE BACK IS IN PLACE, THE ARMS WILL REST ON THESE 3-INCH OVERHANGS.

ASSEMBLING THE STRINGER
■ INSTALLING THE FRONT BRACE

WORKING FROM OUR CUTTING DIAGRAM, WE'VE already cut the front of the stringer with a 75-degree angle. When attaching the front brace to the stringer, make sure you screw it to the stringer's angled edge.

Predrill three holes on either end of the front brace: one in the center (3 5/8 inches in from either edge), and the others 1 5/8 inches in from each edge. (The screw holes should be about 1/2 inch in from the end grain.)

Hold the brace up to the front of the angled end of the stringer and drive your screws home. Do the same for the other end of the front brace. Let the front brace's top edge sit flush with the stringer's longer length. Essentially, you are attaching the front brace to the stringers with six screws, three on each end of the front brace.

You will see that the stringer's end grain is wider than the front brace is tall. You may want to trim or taper the stringer so it matches the front brace's width, though that isn't absolutely necessary (see circled area in photo).

BELOW

SECURE THE FRONT BRACE TO THE STRINGERS WITH THREE SCREWS IN EACH END. THE CIRCLED AREA SHOWS WHERE THE STRINGER IS WIDER THAN THE FRONT BRACE. THOUGH YOU DON'T HAVE TO, YOU CAN TRIM OFF THIS EXCESS WOOD.

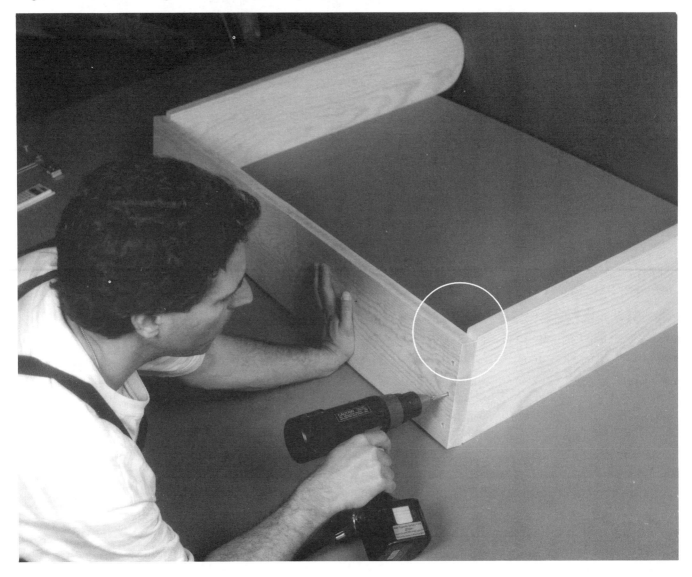

SETTING THE STRINGER ASSEMBLY ON END (WITH the front brace standing straight up and down) makes installing the legs a fairly simple procedure. But the rounded end of the stringer might sag and pull out its screws. To prevent that, insert a temporary spacer between the stringers.

On one of the 24-inch leg pieces you have cut, make a mark at 15 inches. Align the leg flush with the front of the front brace. The top of the front brace should line up with the 15-inch mark. In other words, when your bench is finished and sitting upright, the top of your front brace will sit 15 inches above the ground.

Drill and screw in six screws here, three through the leg and into the end grain of the front brace and three through the leg and into the side of the stringer. As always, stagger these screws slightly to defeat splitting.

Flip the stringer assembly over and repeat the procedure. (You may have to block the rounded end of the stringer with a $^5/4$ scrap, since the leg you just installed will elevate it on one end.)

Now, with both legs installed, set the stringer so it sits like a normal chair, with both front legs on the floor (or work surface). It's time to mark the stringers to show where and at what angle the back will sit.

1 LEFT

SET THE STRINGER ASSEMBLY ON END TO ATTACH THE LEGS, BUT BLOCK THE STRINGER ENDS SO THEY DON'T BOW AND PULL OUT THE FRONT-BRACE SCREWS.

2 ABOVE

POSITION THE LEG SO IT IS FLUSH WITH THE FRONT EDGE OF THE FRONT BRACE. DRIVE THREE SCREWS INTO THE STRINGER AND THREE INTO THE FRONT BRACE'S END GRAIN.

Marking for the Back Placement

We know the angle at which the chair's back will tilt. It's 100 degrees. But where do we mark the guidelines for the back? Where exactly along the stringer will it sit?

Remember, the back has to leave room for the seat slats. Since the seat slats are 3 1/2 inches wide, and there are five of them, we know the seat is at least 17 1/2 inches wide. Add 4 between-slat spaces of, say, 1/8 inch for a total of 1/2 inch, and you'll find that the seat will occupy 18 inches along the top of the stringer.

Thus, the forward-facing part of the back (the part you will actually rest your back against when sitting) should sit 18 inches back from the front of the front brace, where the seat slats start. Measure 18 inches back from the front brace. Make a mark on both stringers.

Put your protractor on the inside of the stringers, set it to 100 degrees, and draw a line along this 100-degree line. This will be the guideline for installing the back.

You may want to increase or decrease the angle of the back. Some people like a 90-degree angle; some people want something more reclining, say, 120 degrees. It's up to you. But if you increase or decrease this angle, it will affect the height of the middle back brace, which will in turn affect the slope of the arms. If you change the angle of the back, be sure to account for it when placing the middle back brace and when cutting the bevels on the front legs and arms supports.

BELOW

USE A PROTRACTOR TO POSITION THE ASSEMBLED BACK PIECE.

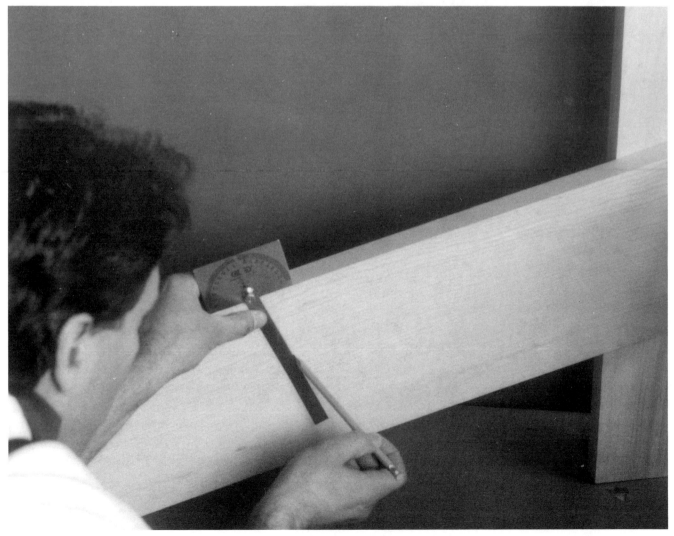

WE ASSEMBLED THE BACK EARLIER (THE SLATS AND braces). Now, we have to position it and screw it into place using the angled guidelines we just drew on the inside of the stringers. Predrill three holes on each stringer so you can easily drive your screws home once the back is properly positioned. Positioning the bench back is a two-, even a three-person job. You need one person (at least) to hold the back in place and one person to drive the screws through the stringers and into the back brace (don't screw into the slats).

Insert the assembled back between the stringers. The front of the back slats should line up with the 100-degree guideline, and the bottom edge of the bottom back brace should line up with the bottom edge of each stringer. Have your helper hold the back in place, and drill and screw three screws for each side. Screw from the outside of the stringer into the bottom back brace (not the slats). Once you have driven the screws in, your assistant can let go of the back.

We have to add some support to the back; otherwise, the six screws would be bearing a lot of the weight of someone sitting on the bench. That's why we have cut some back support blocks. Take the two, 2 x $^5/_4$-inch back support blocks and position them snug up against the bottom back brace. Working from the inside (in between the stringers), drill and screw these blocks into place by screwing sideways into the stringer.

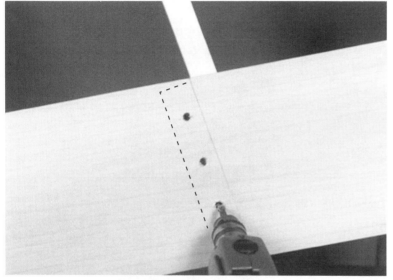

1 ABOVE

USING THE PLACEMENT LINES YOU DREW WITH YOUR PROTRACTOR AS A GUIDE, INSTALL THE BACK. ALIGN THE FRONT EDGE OF THE BACK SLATS WITH THE LINE.

2 LEFT

ONCE THE BACK IS IN PLACE, SCREW A SUPPORT BLOCK BEHIND IT AND INTO EACH STRINGER, USING THREE SCREWS.

INSTALLING THE ARMS

If you've done all your measurements correctly, once you make ¾-inch notches in the middle back brace, the arms should sit level when you lay them in place. Why do we make these notches? Well, since the middle brace is at an angle, we have to create a flat surface on which to screw the arm. If we didn't make the notches, the arms would be sitting on an angled edge of the middle back brace—a weak connection that would soon blow out.

How do you make this notch? How wide and deep should it be?

We want each notch to be about ¾ inches deep, so it provides a good "seat" for the arm to be screwed into. Measure ¾ inches down from the topmost point of the middle brace and make a mark. Then, hold your level up to this mark and draw a level line. This is your depth line.

As for the notch's width, take one of the arms and simply lay it in place. At its rounded end, in the front, have the arm protude 4 inches beyond the leg and overlap it to the inside (over the seat) by a half inch. Then check the other end of the arm (the only remaining square corner), where it touches the back brace. When it's in this position, the arm will naturally rest on the middle back brace where it is supposed to sit, probably ¾ inches away from the outermost back slat. Mark on the middle back brace where the arm is now resting.

We now have the notch's depth and width marked. With a pencil, lightly trace how much wood to remove. Then, with your handsaw make careful cuts to remove this wood. Try to get as close to this line as you can.

When you've finished the cut, take a sharp, 1-inch chisel and shave away the excess wood until you have the notch accurately cut out.

Lay the arm in place, and drill and screw two screws down through the arm into the front leg. Then, drill down and screw two screws into the back brace notch. These

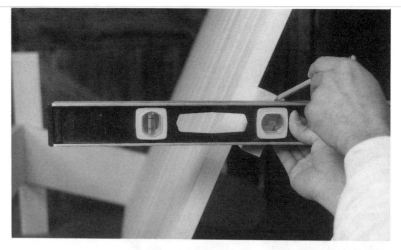

1 ABOVE

Use a level at the end of the middle back brace to mark where to notch out a level pad or "seat" to support the arm.

2 RIGHT

With a handsaw, cut out unwanted wood where the arm will be screwed in place.

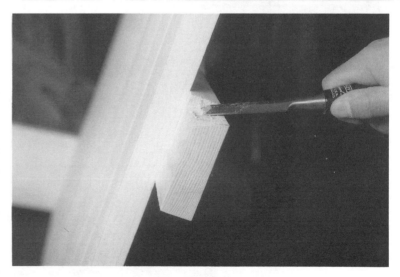

screws must go in at an angle so they do not poke through the outer surface of the brace. With these four screws in place, the arm should feel pretty secure, but there is one more thing to do: install the arm supports.

3 ABOVE

Smooth and level the arm seat with a sharp chisel.

4 ABOVE

ANGLE YOUR
SCREWS WHEN
SCREWING THE
BACK END OF THE
ARM IN PLACE.

5 RIGHT

SECURE THE FRONT
OF THE ARM BY
DRIVING TWO
SCREWS THROUGH
IT AND INTO THE
TOP OF THE LEG.

■ INSTALLING THE ARM SUPPORTS

POSITION AN ARM SUPPORT ON THE OUTSIDE OF a front leg, centering and snugging it up under the arm. It should fit in there square. (If not, the cut on the top of the chair's leg is not square, and the arm is angled, not flat. Or the middle back brace is at the wrong height.)

With this arm support firmly in place, drill and screw from the inside of the front leg into the arm support with three screws. Be sure to position your screws symmetrically so they are centered and equidistant from one other and from the ends of the arm support.

Then, from above, drill and screw two more screws through your arm, down into the arm support.

In the end, there will be five screws in the arm support: two screws driven in from above, through the arm; and three screws driven from the side, through the front leg and into the support.

That's a lot of screws to drive into that little piece of wood. To defeat splitting, do a thorough job of predrilling, and make sure all the screws are centered. If the arm support splits open, it's no big deal. You can make another rather quickly from some scrap ends. The best thing to do is start with a quality piece of wood and carefully drive the screws.

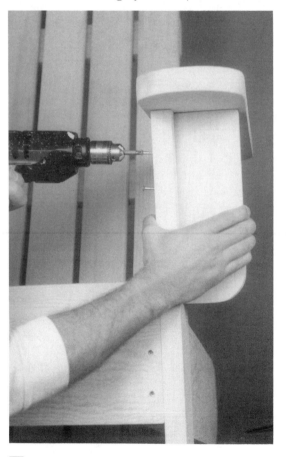

1 ABOVE

FIRST, SECURE THE ARM SUPPORT FROM THE SIDE WITH THREE SCREWS DRIVEN FROM THE INSIDE OF THE LEG.

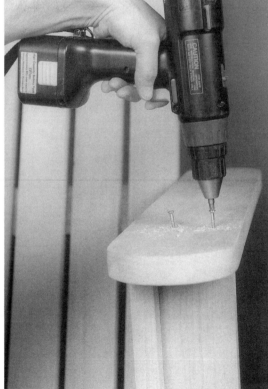

2 ABOVE

NEXT, DRIVE TWO SCREWS DOWN THROUGH THE ARM AND INTO THE TOP OF THE ARM SUPPORT.

Installing the Seat Slats

WELL, YOU'RE GETTING CLOSE NOW! LET'S install the seat slats and wrap this project up.

Lay out all five seat slats and space them evenly so they take up the space between the front brace and the back. You should leave about ¹/₈ inch between each slat. But there are lots of variables here and you may end up leaving more (or less) space, depending on where the chair's back sits. Once you have the seat slats laid out, drill and screw them into place. Do the back one first, then the front one, then fill in between them. Use just one screw for each end of each seat slat.

ABOVE

ATTACH THE SEAT SLATS, USING JUST ONE SCREW FOR EACH SLAT.

A Seat Brace

Since the seat slats span four feet, they might bounce a little when you sit on them. If this bothers you, cut a seat brace and install it at 24 inches, the halfway point. The front of this brace will be a 75-degree angle. The back will be a 100-degree angle. It will be 17 inches long across the top edge. You may have to knock the brace gently into place with a hammer. But once it is in place, screw a block beneath each end to support it.

1 ABOVE

A snug-fitting seat brace, installed at the midpoint of the bench seat slats, adds needed support.

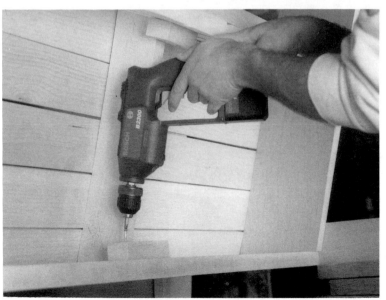

2 LEFT

Blocks screwed into the back side of the stringer and into two of the back slats hold the seat support in place.

1 RIGHT

EPOXY-COATED
WOOD PLUGS CAN
BE TAPPED INTO
PLACE WITH A
HAMMER. MIX THE
EPOXY ON A CAN
LID OR OTHER
CLEAN SURFACE.

2 RIGHT

ONCE THE GLUE IS
COMPLETELY DRY,
SHAVE OFF EXCESS
PLUG WOOD WITH A
RAZOR-SHARP
CHISEL.

3 RIGHT

FINISH BY BELT-
SANDING OR PALM-
SANDING THE
PLUGS, BEING
CAREFUL NOT TO
GOUGE THE WOOD.

IF YOU'VE DRILLED YOUR COUNTERSINKS to the right depth, you should be able to take some 5/16-inch wood plugs, dab them in some glue or epoxy, and tap one in each of the screw holes. (Use pine plugs if you built with pine; oak plugs if you built with oak, and so on.) Be careful when applying the glue that it doesn't overspill onto the wood face of the chair. Yes, you can sand this off, but the wood absorbs some of the glue and when you finish the bench, these areas will take the finish differently.

When tapped into place, the plugs will actually sit just above the surface of the wood. After the glue has dried, belt sand these plugs flush (and then touch up with lighter sandpaper), or take a razor-sharp chisel and cut the top of the plugs flush with the bench's wood surfaces.

■FINAL TOUCH UP

ONCE YOU HAVE THE PLUGS SANDED down, take your palm or pad sander and sand the heck out of the bench. Be careful to remove pencil lines and dirty hand prints. Once you have everything sanded, flip ahead to chapter 10 for more tips on finishing your work with sealant, urethane, or paint.

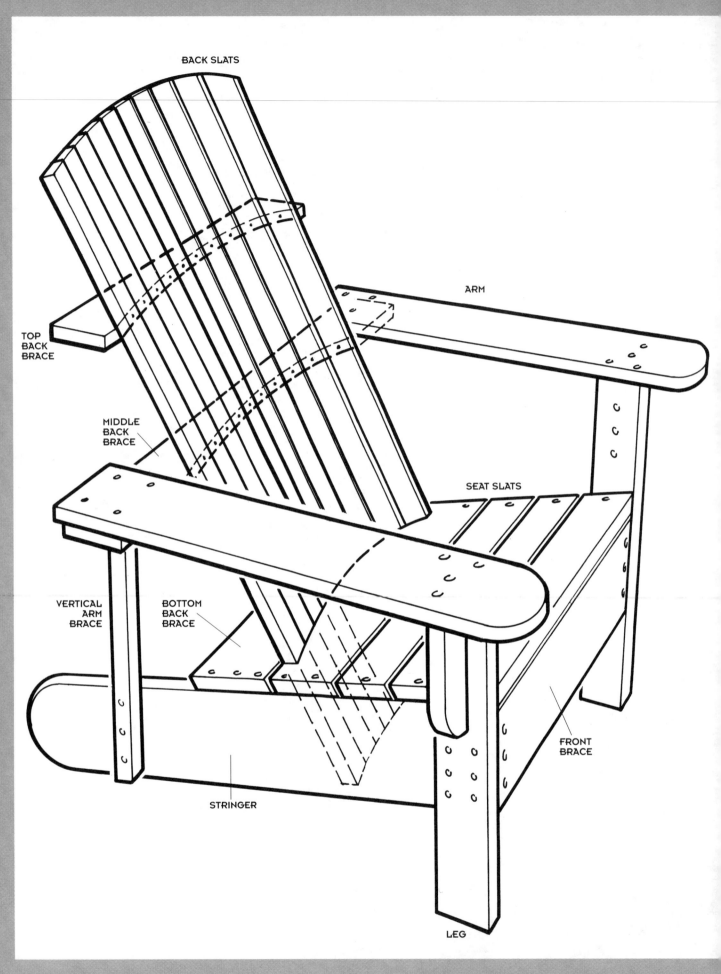

BACK SLATS

ARM

TOP
BACK
BRACE

MIDDLE
BACK
BRACE

SEAT SLATS

VERTICAL
ARM
BRACE

BOTTOM
BACK
BRACE

FRONT
BRACE

STRINGER

LEG

6
BUILDING A SCALLOP-BACK CHAIR OR BENCH

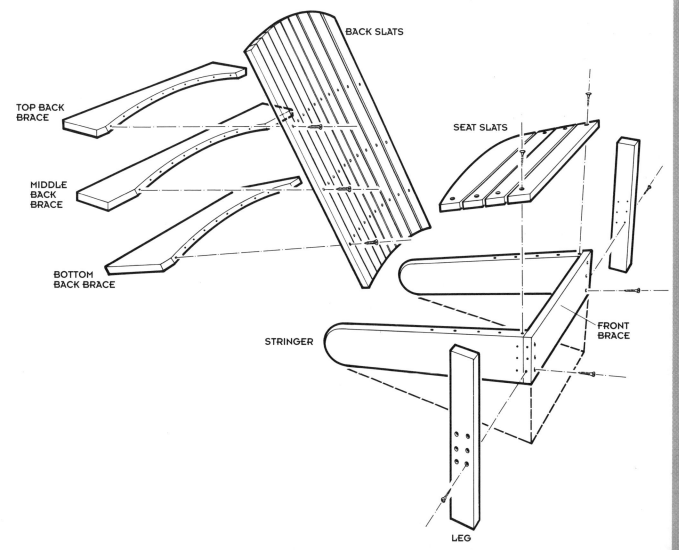

BACK SLATS

TOP BACK
BRACE

SEAT SLATS

MIDDLE
BACK
BRACE

BOTTOM
BACK BRACE

FRONT
BRACE

STRINGER

LEG

SOME OF YOU may want to modify your chair or bench to give it a scalloped, or contoured, back. The back on such a chair curves slightly to wrap around you as you sit. It's a popular design, and, though not as true to the original Adirondack tradition as the straight-backed chair and bench featured in this book, it's very comfortable and not that difficult to make. Its design is slightly different from the ones I've shown so far, but, with some small modifications and a few curved cuts, you can create a scallop-back Adirondack chair or bench using the plans for our straight-back models as a basis.

You can see on page 88 how the scallop-back chair differs from its straight-backed cousin— the cross braces at the top, middle, and bottom of the back slats are boards that rest on their sides. You'll also notice that each is cut with a curved line. By contrast, the cross braces on a straight-back chair run flat against the back slats.

Next, you'll see that, on each side of the chair, there is a vertical brace running from the stringer to the underside of the arm. Why do we need these reinforcements? Well, with the cross braces resting on their sides, we can no longer depend on them for the support they once offered when positioned flat. The vertical braces compensate for this support deficiency.

You'll also notice that there are eleven back slats, (we used five in our straight-back chair). That's because the back slats are thinner (either 2x2s or $5/4$ x 4s ripped in half lengthwise). Wider slats would bridge the curve and flatten it, defeating the scalloping effect (see page 39).

Finally, notice that the seat slat closest to the back slats is *scribed*, or cut to fit within the curved back, and that it's a wider board (we'll use a $5/4$ x 8 here).

There is one real trick to cutting the boards for this scallop-back chair: the cross braces on the back have to be cut with a jigsaw, not only to create the curve, but also to create an angled line against which the back slats will rest flush. This angle will match the angle of the back, or 100 degrees (see opposite page). How do you cut this angled curve? For starters, refer back to chapter 3 for instructions on how to mark a curved line, but now when you cut, use a jigsaw that can be set at an angle (the base or *sole plate* of the saw can be tilted). Set the saw's sole plate at 65 degrees for the middle and top braces (For the bottom back brace, set the saw's sole plate at 80 degrees.) That way, you'll be cutting a curved, angled line. It might be tricky for you if you've never done one before, so practice first on a throwaway board to avoid making mistakes on your good lumber.

Here's a general, step-by-step approach to building this scallop-back chair. I'm going to assume that you know the basic marking and cutting techniques from the other chapters in this book, and that you'll use the same countersink-and-screw method for attaching the boards to one another.

First, the arms, arm supports, stringers, front brace, and front legs are

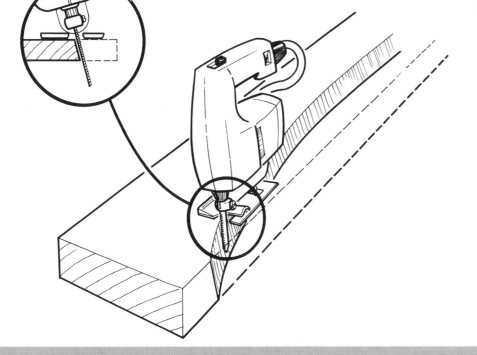

all exactly the same components we presented in chapters 3, 4, and 5. You can cut these and set them aside.

When installing the back for a straight-back chair, we preassembled it on the workbench. We won't be doing that here. Instead, we'll put the bottom back brace in place on the stringers and then attach the back slats to it.

Also, for our straight-back chair, we were able to screw from the back braces into the back of the back slats. Here, since the braces are much wider, we'll start our screws from the *front* side of the back braces, screwing through them and into the back braces. After these screw holes are plugged, sanded, and finished, they won't be uncomfortable to rest against, because the plugs will be flush with the back braces' surfaces. Still, if you don't like the idea of seeing plugged screw heads from the front side of your chair, you can screw in from the back. You'll just have to use properly countersink 6-inch screws and make sure they reach all the way through the back brace and substantially into the back of the back slats.

■CUTTING THE BACK BRACES FOR A SCALLOP-BACK CHAIR

LET'S START BY CUTTING OUR three back braces. What dimension lumber should we use? Since cutting the curved lines removes a great deal of material, we'll use $5/4$ x 6 stock boards—nothing less—for the middle and top back braces. The bottom back brace will be $5/4$ x 8 stock, as it is in our straight-back chair.

The bottom back brace will not sit between the stringers as it does for our straight-back chair, but, rather, on top of them. Thus, make the bottom back brace the same length as your seat slats: 23 inches. Once you've cut the board to length, you can mark the curved line that will create the scallop. What radius should you use? Well, that depends on how deep you want the curve in the back to go. I suggest a subtle curve, with an apex of 3 inches. When drawing the curve, don't start at the edge of the brace. The curve has to start from a point flush with the inner edge of the stringer to accomodate the back slats, so start drawing your curve $1\frac{1}{8}$ inches in from each end of the brace.

The middle back

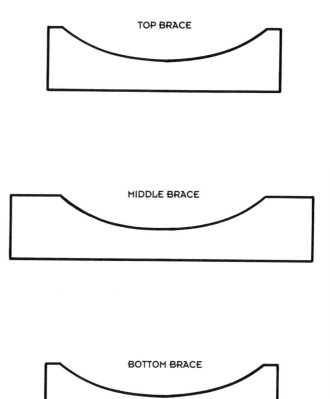

brace needs the exact same curve cut into it. But once positioned, this brace must also be long enough at either end to support the chair's arms. Our straight-back chair had a middle brace $26\frac{3}{4}$ inches long. We'll make this one 29 inches so that it supports more than half the width of the arms. On this 29-inch board mark a curved line identical to the one you just marked on the bottom back brace. Be sure to position the curve so that its 3-inch apex is at the board's very center.

The top back brace can be shorter than the middle brace, since it supports no arms, only the back slats themselves (in fact, some people don't install a top brace at all). This brace can be just the width of the back slats plus an inch on either side where the board's square lines meet its curved lines. So, cut it the same length as the bottom back brace: 23 inches.

When you have all three back braces marked and cut with a properly set jigsaw, you are ready to assemble the back.

■ ASSEMBLING YOUR SCALLOP-BACK CHAIR

FIRST, ASSEMBLE THE FRONT legs, stringer, and front brace just as you would for the straight-back chair (see pages 50-51). Now lay your bottom back brace on *top of* the stringers so that its front edge is 18 inches back from the front edge of the front brace. The 80-degree angle of the back brace should slope away from the front brace so that when you install your chair's back slats they slope back properly. Screw this brace in place with three screws on either side, screwing down through the brace and into the stringers.

The next step is a little tricky, because you have to do two things at once (call your helper here!). First, on your workbench, attach the middle back brace to the underside of the arms. Set the arms on the middle brace so the inside edge of the arms sits just 1 inch from where the curve starts and so its 65-degree angle will maintain the slope established by the bottom brace. The assembly should look like a big wooden horse-shoe (see below).

Back at your stringer assembly, install two back slats at either end of the bottom back brace. Screw them into the back brace and into the stringer so that their butt ends are flush with the stringer's bottom edge. When screwing them into the stringer, work from the inside out, so you won't see the screw holes in the finished product. The two back slats should now be sticking up in the air at the correct angle established by the bottom back brace (see drawing at top of opposite page). Now, lay the wooden horseshoe (the arm-and-brace assembly)

in place on top of the front legs. Have your helper hold it in place. Put a level on one of the arms. Raise or lower the back end of the arm and brace assembly until the arms are level. When you've positioned them level, screw through the back slats and into the middle back brace (one screw per slat will do).

Now install the rest of the back slats, with even spacing between them. The bottom edge of these slats should be flush with the bottom edge of the bottom back brace. When you have all the back slats in place, install your top back brace 8 inches down from the top of the back slats. Screw through the back slat and into the top back brace, one screw per slat (see drawing at bottom of opposite page).

We're almost done. Let's get our vertical supports in place to add more stability to the chair.

Using back-slat stock (2x2s or $5/4$ x 4 ripped lengthwise in half), hold a 22-inch vertical brace in place, butted up against the underside of the arm and flush against the outside of the stringer. (Trim it to

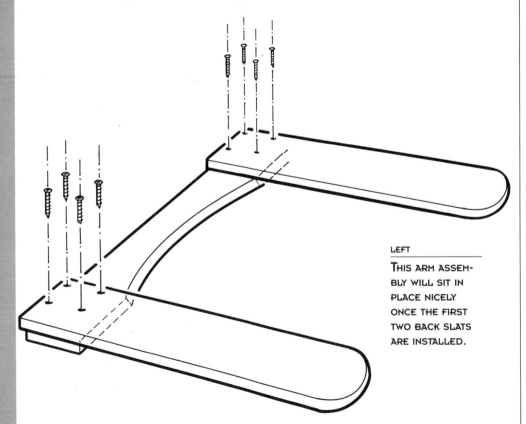

LEFT

THIS ARM ASSEM-
BLY WILL SIT IN
PLACE NICELY
ONCE THE FIRST
TWO BACK SLATS
ARE INSTALLED.

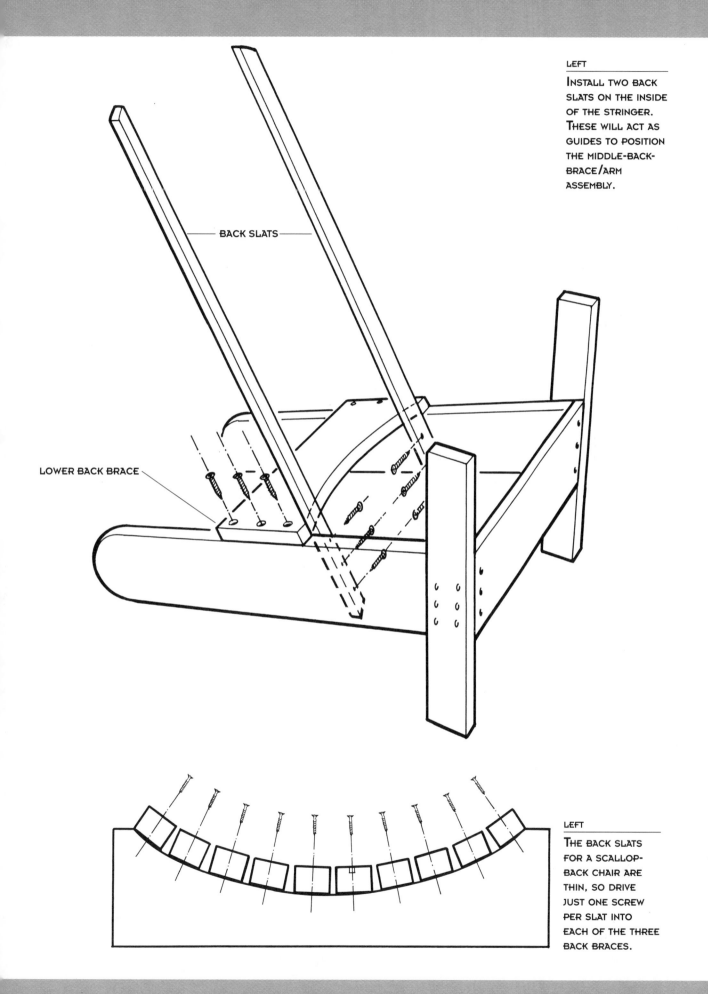

BACK SLATS

LEFT

INSTALL TWO BACK
SLATS ON THE INSIDE
OF THE STRINGER.
THESE WILL ACT AS
GUIDES TO POSITION
THE MIDDLE-BACK-
BRACE/ARM
ASSEMBLY.

LOWER BACK BRACE

LEFT

THE BACK SLATS
FOR A SCALLOP-
BACK CHAIR ARE
THIN, SO DRIVE
JUST ONE SCREW
PER SLAT INTO
EACH OF THE THREE
BACK BRACES.

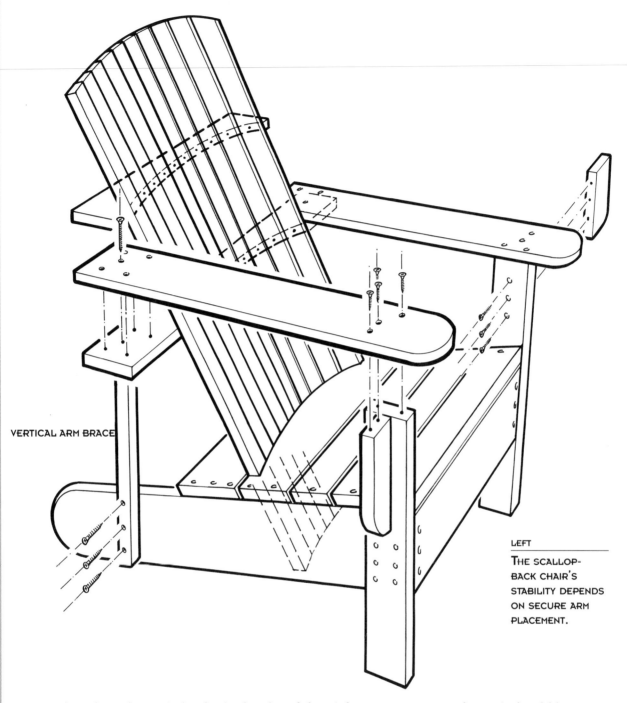

VERTICAL ARM BRACE

proper length so that it covers the full width of the stringer.) Place a level on it to make sure it is *plumb* (perfectly vertical). Then, use three screws to secure it to the stringer and drive an additional screw down through the arm into the top of the vertical brace. Do

this for both sides of the chair, so that a single vertical brace supports each arm.

Next, you must scribe that first seat slat. You'll notice that if you put in a square-cut $5/4$ x 4 seat slat, it would leave a big, curving gap between its back edge and the back slats. So, we scribe it to

fit, cutting a curve that matches the contour of the back. Use a $5/4$ x 8 board so that you can cut out the necessary material and so the rest of the seat slats space evenly (a x 8 is nearly the equivalent of two x 4s) and you won't have to rip any odd-size slats. Note: This scribed slat

should be cut at an 80-degree angle with your jigsaw.

When the seat slat is scribed, fit it in place and screw it down. Then, install the remaining seat slats as you normally would, with one screw on each end of each slat (see page 57).

RIGHT

A VERTICAL BRACE RUNNING FROM THE STRINGER TO THE UNDERSIDE OF THE ARMS IS ESSENTIAL FOR ADDITIONAL SUPPORT.

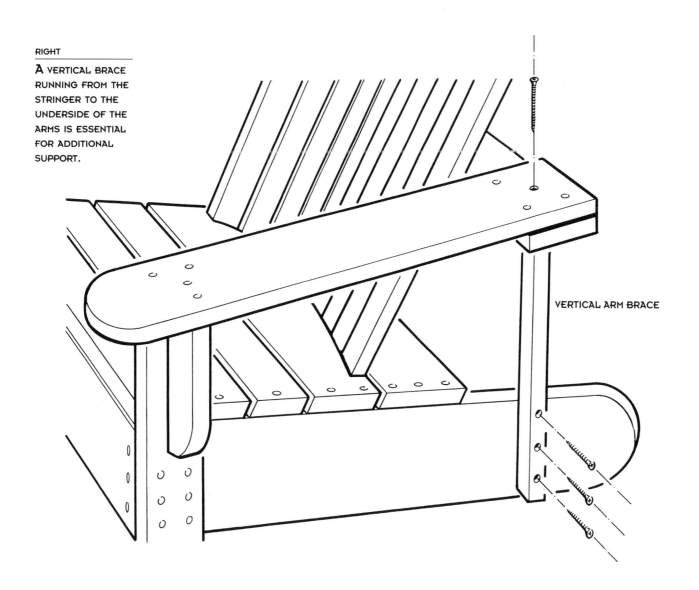

VERTICAL ARM BRACE

■ FINISHING YOUR SCALLOP-BACK CHAIR

AS WITH THE STRAIGHT-back Adirondack chair, the back slats for the scallop-back model can be marked with a curve and cut (see chapter 9). And if you want to get fancy with the back curves, chapter 9 includes some suggested designs.

Once your chair is assembled and you've made your cuts, it's time to start sanding, plug-ging, and choosing a finish coat (see chapter 10 for information on this latter subject).

■ MAKING A SCALLOP-BACK BENCH

WANT TO MAKE A SCALLOP-back bench? No prob-lem. Follow the steps for the scallop-back chair, but be sure to account for the longer lengths of the seat slats. The assembly procedures are the same. You may want to use a larger radius on the curve for the three back braces or cut individual sets of scallops for two bench users. You can do either. Just be careful not to cut more than half the width out of any of the back braces and be sure to cut the curves (for the top and middle braces) at 65-degree angles and the bottom back brace at an 80-degree angle.

BUILDING THE TABLE

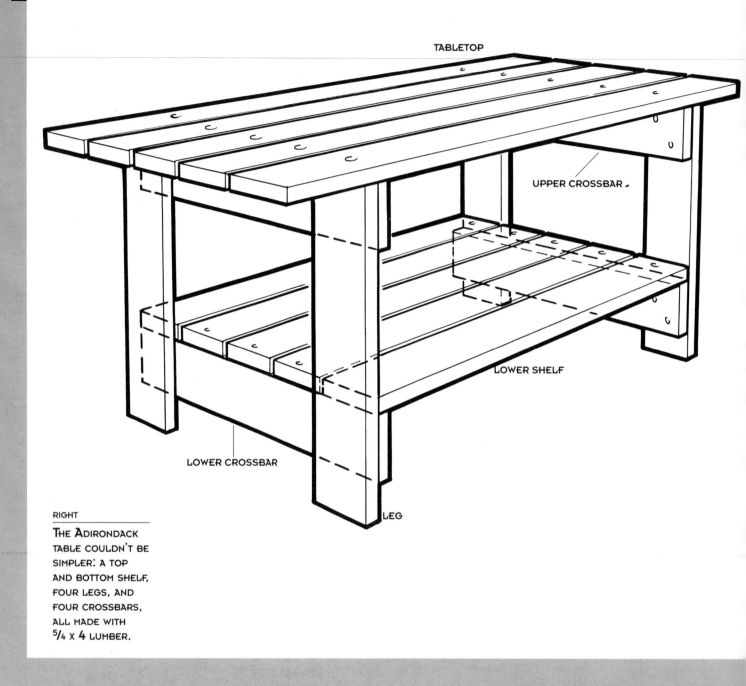

TABLETOP

UPPER CROSSBAR

LOWER SHELF

LOWER CROSSBAR

LEG

THE ADIRONDACK
TABLE COULDN'T BE
SIMPLER: A TOP
AND BOTTOM SHELF,
FOUR LEGS, AND
FOUR CROSSBARS,
ALL MADE WITH
$^5/_4$ x 4 LUMBER.

THIS TABLE IS EASY TO BUILD AND WILL MAKE A FINE
addition to your Adirondack furniture set.
Whether you plan on setting up your newly built
furniture on a back porch, in a greenhouse, or
out on the lawn, a matching table will come in handy as a
place to set down a tray of drinks and hors d'oeuvres or
that unfinished crossword puzzle. In fact, the furniture set
will not be complete without a table. So here's how to put
one together.

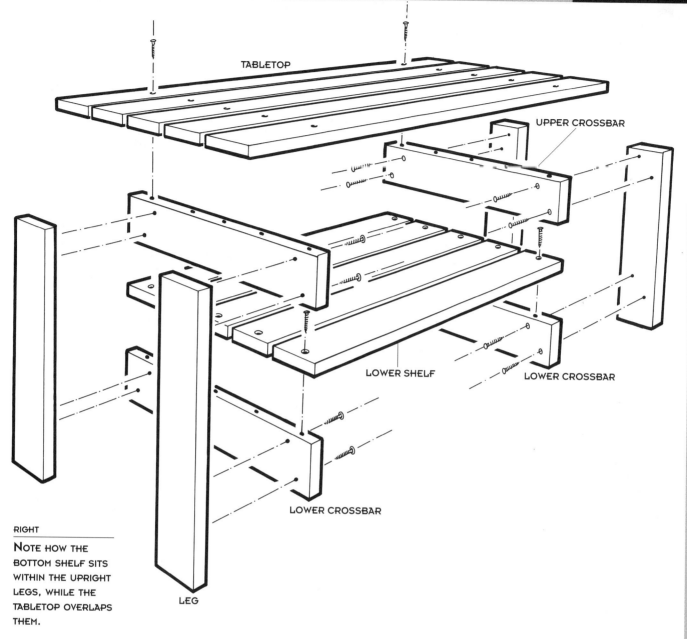

TABLETOP

UPPER CROSSBAR

LOWER SHELF

LOWER CROSSBAR

LOWER CROSSBAR

LEG

RIGHT

Note how the bottom shelf sits within the upright legs, while the tabletop overlaps them.

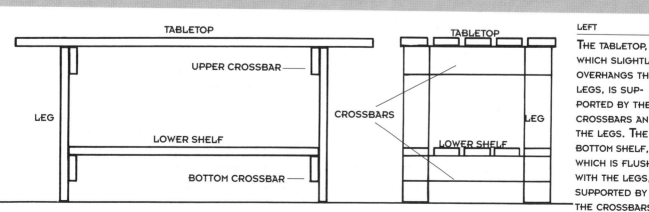

TABLETOP

UPPER CROSSBAR

LEG

LOWER SHELF

BOTTOM CROSSBAR

TABLETOP

CROSSBARS

LEG

LOWER SHELF

LEFT

The tabletop, which slightly overhangs the legs, is supported by the crossbars and the legs. The bottom shelf, which is flush with the legs, is supported by the crossbars.

GETTING READY

Cut and sand all the pieces of wood from the cut list into the lengths marked on the cutting diagram. If you need help with cutting techniques, refer back to chapter 3 to freshen your memory. If you have built any other piece of furniture in this book, the same principles of measurement, cutting techniques, and safety apply for the table as well.

As with our other projects, try to work with two drills. Though one will do, two drills are more convenient, because you won't have to stop and change bits every time you want to drive screws into place.

In any event use a variable-speed drill. Load it with a #8 countersink/predrill bit. Whenever you insert a screw, it must be through a predrilled hole that has been drilled out with this countersink. The predrilled hole helps stop the wood from splitting, and the countersink allows the head of the screw to sit below the surface of the board. (We'll fill these countersink holes with wood plugs later.) If you were to drive your screws without predrilling or countersinking the hole, the wood might split with the wedge action of the screw, and the head of the screw would sit flush with the surface of the wood. Besides being unsightly, the flush screw head also prevents you from plugging the hole, which is essential for keeping water out.

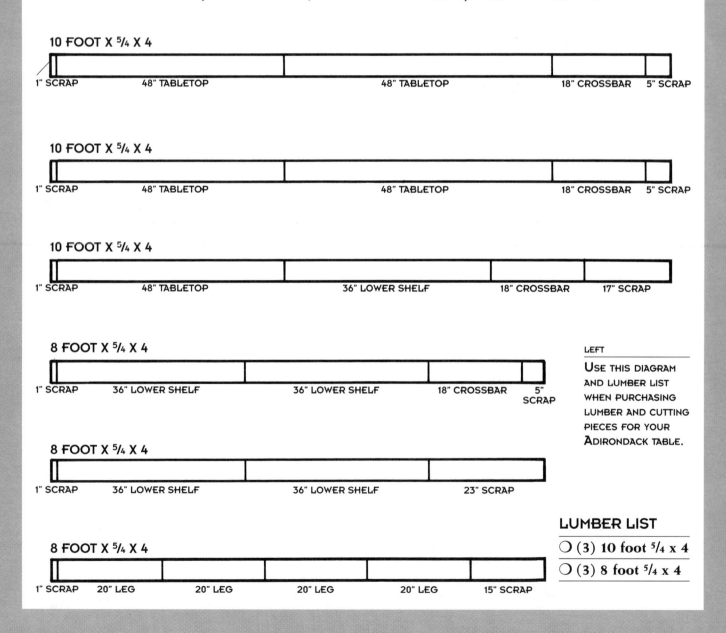

10 FOOT X $^5/_4$ X 4

1" SCRAP   48" TABLETOP   48" TABLETOP   18" CROSSBAR   5" SCRAP

10 FOOT X $^5/_4$ X 4

1" SCRAP   48" TABLETOP   48" TABLETOP   18" CROSSBAR   5" SCRAP

10 FOOT X $^5/_4$ X 4

1" SCRAP   48" TABLETOP   36" LOWER SHELF   18" CROSSBAR   17" SCRAP

8 FOOT X $^5/_4$ X 4

1" SCRAP   36" LOWER SHELF   36" LOWER SHELF   18" CROSSBAR   5" SCRAP

8 FOOT X $^5/_4$ X 4

1" SCRAP   36" LOWER SHELF   36" LOWER SHELF   23" SCRAP

8 FOOT X $^5/_4$ X 4

1" SCRAP   20" LEG   20" LEG   20" LEG   20" LEG   15" SCRAP

LEFT

USE THIS DIAGRAM AND LUMBER LIST WHEN PURCHASING LUMBER AND CUTTING PIECES FOR YOUR ADIRONDACK TABLE.

LUMBER LIST

- ○ (3) 10 foot $^5/_4$ x 4
- ○ (3) 8 foot $^5/_4$ x 4

WE'LL START OUR TABLE ASSEMBLY WITH THE LEGS and crossbars. Once we stand the legs up, we can lay in the lower shelf and screw it down. Then we'll put the table top on and screw it down. We'll install the lower shelf first, because trying to install it after the tabletop is in place would be an awkward business.

Start with two 20-inch legs and lay them down on your work surface. Use a framing square or similar tool to establish that they are square to each other and 18 inches apart. Now, lay the top crossbar across these legs. The crossbar is 18 inches long, so it should come square and flush to the outside and top of the legs.

Drill and screw two #8 1½-inch wood screws through the crossbar into the leg beneath it. Drive the screws in a diagonal pattern and make sure they are at least 1 inch from the edge of the board. Then drive two screws through the other end of the crossbar and into the leg beneath it.

Before installing the bottom crossbar, make sure that the legs are 18 inches apart down their full length. You don't want the legs to be *racked* (unsquare).

Install the bottom crossbar so that its top edge is 6 inches up from the end of the leg (the part of the leg that will rest on the ground). This means that when the bottom shelf is screwed in place, it will be about 7¼ inches above the ground.

If you want to change the height of the lower shelf, now is the time to raise or lower the bottom crossbar. The height of the lower shelf will not affect the stability of the design. (Leaving the lower shelf out altogether, on the other hand, would make for a slightly unstable table.)

Once you have the bottom crossbar square and in place, drill and screw it to the legs. Use two screws for each leg. Screw down through the crossbar and into the leg beneath it.

Use the same procedure to lay out and install the crossbars on the other two legs so you have two sets of legs. It may not look like a table yet, but we've just finished assembling the legs. Let's move on to installing the lower shelf.

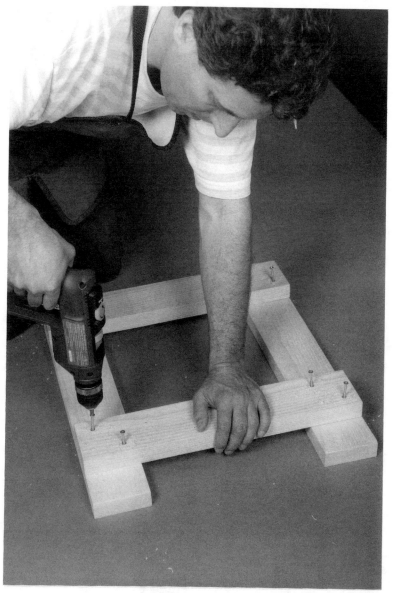

LEFT

SQUARE UP ALL THE WOOD PIECES FOR YOUR LEG ASSEMBLY BEFORE SCREWING ANY OF THEM DOWN.

AT 20 INCHES WIDE, OUR TABLETOP will be 2 inches wider than the lower shelf. Even though we will use the same number of slats for both surfaces, we are going to set them more tightly together on the lower shelf. We are using five slats, each one 3 1/2 inches wide (regular 5/4 x 4s), and we will set them just 1/8 inch apart for the lower shelf. (For the tabletop, we will set them just over 1/2 inch apart.)

If you stand up one leg-and-crossbar assembly and place one slat on the bottom crossbar, you can screw it in place. But what do you do with the other end of the slat? You can't raise and stabilize *both* leg assemblies at once. So, prop the other end of the slat on a block at crossbar height, then position your slat on one leg assembly. Or have someone hold the slat while you screw it in place.

Square the shelf slat to one end of the bottom crossbar. The outside edge of the shelf slat should be flush with the outside edge of the crossbar. Since the slat is long, it's easy to install it askew—you may want to position it with the help of a framing square. When the shelf slat is square and flush to the crossbar, drill and screw it in place with two screws (see below).

Now stand up the other leg assembly, and screw the shelf slats in place into that leg assembly. Now the leg assemblies will stand on their own while we install the other shelf slats. Install the other outside shelf slat at the other end of the crossbar.

Drop the other shelf slats in between the two outer ones we just installed. Space them evenly and drill and screw them in place.

2 ABOVE

SCREW THE OUTSIDE SHELF PIECES IN PLACE FIRST, AND THEN FILL IN THE SPACE BETWEEN THEM WITH THE OTHER SLATS.

1 BELOW

SCREW THE LOWER SHELF INTO THE LOWER CROSSBAR OF THE LEG ASSEMBLY.

3 LEFT

MAKE SURE ALL
OF THE MIDDLE
THREE SHELF
SLATS ARE EVENLY
POSITIONED
BEFORE SCREWING
ANY OF THEM
DOWN.

Installing the Tabletop

Before installing the tabletop, recheck the distance between the legs, end to end. You want the legs to be as far apart at the bottom (where they touch the floor) as they are on the top (where we're about to install the table top slats). Otherwise, the table will be wobbly, and the top not level.

Take a tabletop slat and lay it in place so its edge overhangs the leg assembly by ½ inch. Be sure that your tabletop slat is square to the leg assembly, even though it overhangs it. Use a framing square to check this.

Also, the tabletop slat will protrude 5 inches at either end of the table, because the tabletop slats are a foot longer than the lower shelf. Drill and screw this first slat in place with two screws through each end of the slat. Screw down through the slat and into the crossbar.

Repeat this exact procedure on the other side of the table. Install this second tabletop slat so it overhangs the leg assembly by ½ inch and protrudes beyond the leg assembly by 5 inches at either end. When it's square, screw it down.

With these two outer legs in place, lay out the remaining three tabletop slats between them and space them evenly. Drill and screw these slats into place. Use two screws for each end of the slats.

With the tabletop slats all screwed in place, the table is done.

 RIGHT

TABLETOP SHOULD
PROTRUDE 5 INCHES
BEYOND THE LEGS.
USING A SQUARE,
POSITION THE
OUTSIDE SLATS FIRST.

2 ABOVE

POSITION THE MIDDLE THREE TABLETOP SLATS WITH A SQUARE SO THAT THEY ALSO OVERHANG THE LEGS BY 5 INCHES.

3 LEFT

POSITION ALL THREE MIDDLE TABLETOP SLATS BEFORE SCREWING ANY OF THEM DOWN.

PLUGGING THE SCREW HOLES

JUST AS WITH THE OTHER ADIRONDACK furniture you might have made from this book, we are going to plug the screw holes with pine plugs, glued in place.

If you've drilled your countersinks to the right depth, you should be able to take some 5/16-inch plugs, dab them in some glue or epoxy, and tap one into each screw hole. Be careful when applying the glue that it doesn't spill over onto the wood face of the chair. You can sand off most of the glue, but the wood will absorb some of it and take the finish (oil, polyurethane, paint) differently in those places.

After the glue is dry, belt-sand these plugs flush with the tabletop, or take a razor-sharp, 1-inch wood chisel and cut them flush with the table. Then, touch-sand these plugs with a palm or pad sander.

LEFT

PLACE EPOXY-DIPPED WOOD PLUGS INTO THE COUNTERSINK HOLES. MIX THE EPOXY ON A CAN TOP OR OTHER CLEAN SURFACE.

SAND, SAND, SAND

WHEN YOU'RE DONE ASSEMBLING THE TABLE, SAND the heck out of it with #120 and then #220 sandpaper. Sand off any pencil marks or marks left by dirty hands. Then, flip ahead to chapter 10 for information on sealing, finishing, or painting your table.

BUILDING THE LEG REST

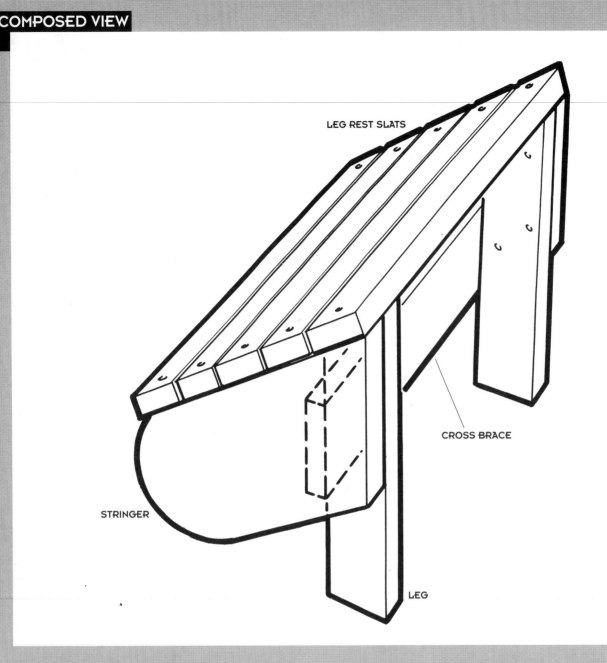

LEG REST SLATS

CROSS BRACE

STRINGER

LEG

BUILDING THE LEG REST CAN CHANGE YOUR ADIRONDACK CHAIR INTO a chaise. The leg rest won't be attached to the Adirondack chair. It will be separate, like an ottoman. However, if you compare the Adirondack chair to the leg rest shown here, you'll see that the top of the leg rest and the chair's seat are at the same height. You don't need a math degree to know that this means your legs can comfortably fall across the leg rest and chair at once. You won't be able to detect that they are two separate pieces of furniture. They are built to match.

As for the folks who'll use the bench you built, you could build a 48-inch-wide double leg rest (though it would be rather unwieldy). The better solution, though, is to build two single leg rests, one for each side of the bench.

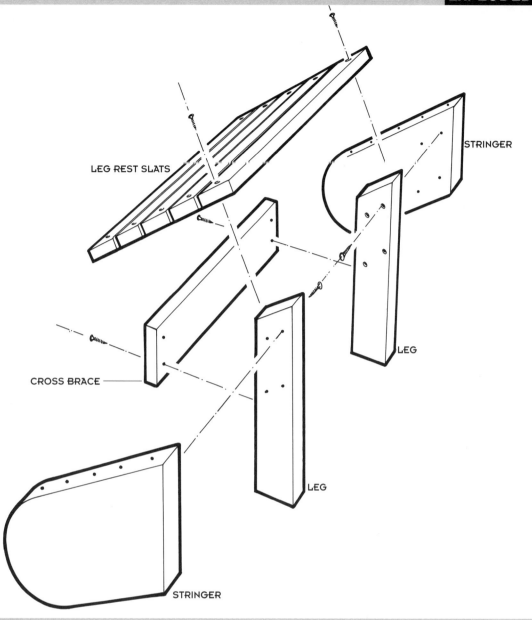

LEG REST SLATS

STRINGER

CROSS BRACE

LEG

LEG

STRINGER

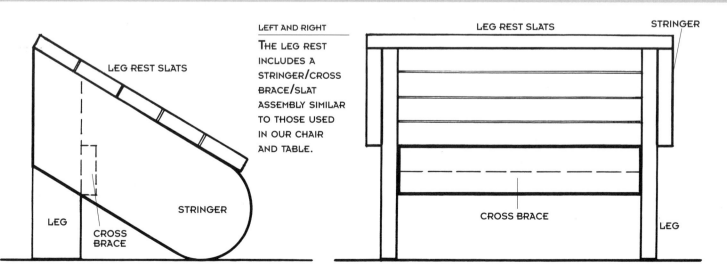

LEG REST SLATS

LEFT AND RIGHT
THE LEG REST INCLUDES A STRINGER/CROSS BRACE/SLAT ASSEMBLY SIMILAR TO THOSE USED IN OUR CHAIR AND TABLE.

LEG REST SLATS

STRINGER

STRINGER

LEG

CROSS BRACE

CROSS BRACE

LEG

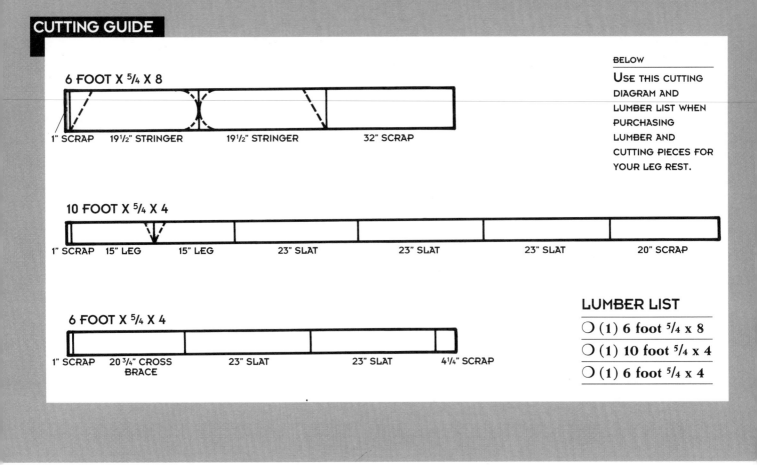

BELOW

USE THIS CUTTING DIAGRAM AND LUMBER LIST WHEN PURCHASING LUMBER AND CUTTING PIECES FOR YOUR LEG REST.

6 FOOT X ⁵/₄ X 8

1" SCRAP | 19¹/₂" STRINGER | 19¹/₂" STRINGER | 32" SCRAP

10 FOOT X ⁵/₄ X 4

1" SCRAP | 15" LEG | 15" LEG | 23" SLAT | 23" SLAT | 23" SLAT | 20" SCRAP

6 FOOT X ⁵/₄ X 4

1" SCRAP | 20³/₄" CROSS BRACE | 23" SLAT | 23" SLAT | 4¹/₄" SCRAP

LUMBER LIST

◯ (1) 6 foot ⁵/₄ x 8
◯ (1) 10 foot ⁵/₄ x 4
◯ (1) 6 foot ⁵/₄ x 4

ASSEMBLING THE LEG REST

AFTER YOU'VE CUT AND SANDED ALL THE PIECES of wood from the cut list into the lengths marked on the cutting diagram, gather them near your work surface. As with our other projects, it's best to have two variable speed drills handy (though one will do fine). Load one with a #8 countersink predrill, and the other with a Phillips drive bit.

If you followed the cutting diagram, you cut your stringers with a 60-degree angle. This will cause your 19 ¹/₂-inch long stringers to slope down at, what I think, is a com-fortable angle. (You may want more or less slope to your leg rest. In that case, increase the angle for a more gentle slope, and decrease the angle for a more radical drop. You will find, however, that you have to adjust the length of your stringer accordingly.)

The curves on the stringer's lower ends have a 3 ¹/₂-inch radius, just like those we cut on the chair and bench stringers. If you need to refresh your memory on how to cut these, refer to chapter 3, "Marking and Cutting Curves," page 32-33.

DESIRED LEG-REST ANGLE	STRINGER LENGTH REQUIRED
60 degrees	19 ¹/₂ inches
65 degrees	23 inches
70 degrees	28 ³/₄ inches
75 degrees	34 ¹/₄ inches
80 degrees	44 ¹/₂ inches

Unlike the Adirondack chair or bench, we are going to attach our rest's legs to the stringers before we do anything else. You have already cut the legs so that one end has a 60-degree angle. The leg should stand 15 inches tall at the high point of the angle.

Lay one of the legs so that its 60-degree angle lies flush with the top of the stringer. Square the leg to the stringer's front edge. Once the leg is in place, drill and screw four #8 1 ½-inch wood screws through the leg and into the stringer.

Repeat this procedure on the other stringer, giving you two stringer-and-leg assemblies. But watch out! Look at the photo here. The assemblies must mirror each other, with the legs positioned on what will be the *inside* of the stringers. We will next install the leg-rest slats and cross brace to hold these two stringers together.

1 RIGHT

THE STRINGER-AND-LEG ASSEMBLIES FOR THE LEG REST SHOULD MIRROR EACH OTHER.

2 BELOW

ONCE YOU HAVE THE LEGS ALL LINED UP WITH THE STRINGER, SCREW DOWN THROUGH THE LEG AND INTO THE STRINGER BENEATH. USE FOUR SCREWS.

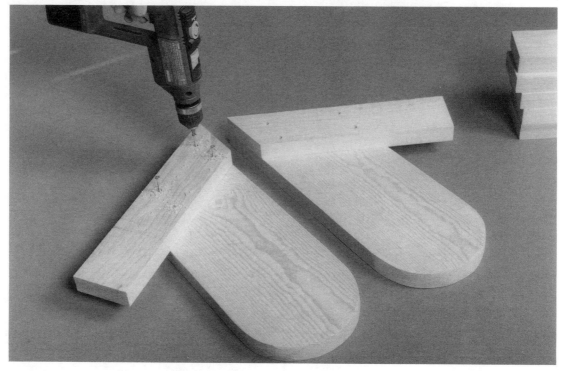

INSTALLING THE SLATS AND BRACE

IF THE LEG REST SLATS WERE YOUR ONLY bracing, the leg rest might rack, because there's nothing across the bottom of the legs to hold them square. To solve this problem, we are going to install a cross brace. But, first, to help hold everything together we will install one leg rest.

Lay one leg-rest slat across the top of the stringers, where it will meet the chair's seat. Predrill the screw holes. Set the slat in place so it is flush to the outside of the stringers and screw it in place. The stringer assembly may be a bit wobbly with only one slat in place. But we'll now have an easier time installing the cross brace.

Flip the leg rest over so that the legs are resting on the work surface. Take your 20 3/4-inch cross brace and position it so its bottom edge is right where the stringers and legs intersect. Screw it into place with two screws at either end. You will be driving the screws through the brace and into the back (edge) surface of the legs.

Flip the leg rest upright and install the remaining four leg-rest slats. Our first slat is already in place, so lay the others snugly against each other. Put one screw at either end of these slats, just as you did on the chair's seat slats. You will find that the last slat slightly overhangs the curved part of the stringer. Be sure to glue this last slat especially well, as it will take a lot of wear and tear. (You might even want to drive a second screw at either end of this last slat.)

1 ABOVE

A CROSS BRACE INSTALLED ON THE BACK OF THE LEGS ADDS ESSENTIAL STABILITY TO THE LEG REST.

2 BELOW

ONCE YOU HAVE THE LEGS ATTACHED AND THE CROSS BRACE INSTALLED, SCREW DOWN THE LEG-REST SLATS, USING ONE SCREW FOR EACH.

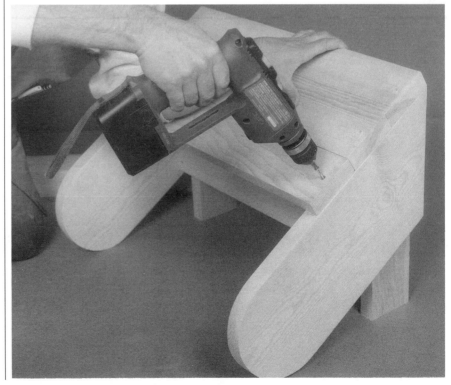

PLUG AND SAND

ONCE THE LEG REST IS COMPLETE, PLUG the screw holes with 5/16-inch plugs, belt-sanding or chiseling them flush, then touch-sanding the plug tops with #100 sandpaper.

Now sand the heck out of the leg rest with #120 and #220 sandpaper. Sand out any pencil marks or dirty hand prints. When the piece is completely sanded, flip ahead to chapter 10 for tips on painting or sealing it.

FANCY-CUTTING THE BACK SLATS

9

113
One
Consistent
Curve

114
Multiple
Curves

THE BACK SLATS ON YOUR CHAIR OR bench can be cut a number of ways to add character to your furniture. Not that your Adirondack furniture doesn't have lots of character already! Fancy cuts will just add a bit more.

Of course, you can just leave the back slats square, all the same length. That look has its own appeal. It's simple; the lines are clean, plus you don't have to get nervous making a jigsaw cut into the back of the perfect chair you just spent a weekend building. But if you want to add some designs, you can draw curved lines to cut with your jigsaw.

Shown here are some back-slat design options for both the bench and chair. Take a look at them and see if one appeals to you. If not, make up a pattern of your own. But re-member, there are an odd number of back slats (5 on the chair and 11 on the bench). Be sure you account for the center slat if you create a symmetrical design.

All of the back-slat designs suggested here can be drawn using the "pencil-on-a-string" technique. Here's how it works.

Tie a sharpened pencil at one end of a 3-foot length of string. Wherever you place the other end of the string establishes the center of a circle. If you trap that end of the string under your thumb, gently pull the string taut, and swing the pencil, it will draw an arc. Try it on your chair and bench backs. Pin the string under your thumb somewhere along the base of the center back slat and use the pencil to draw an arc (your cut line) along the top of all the slats.

1 BELOW

A PENCIL ON THE END OF A STRING CAN BE USED TO MAKE CURVED LINES ALONG THE TOP OF THE BACK SLATS.

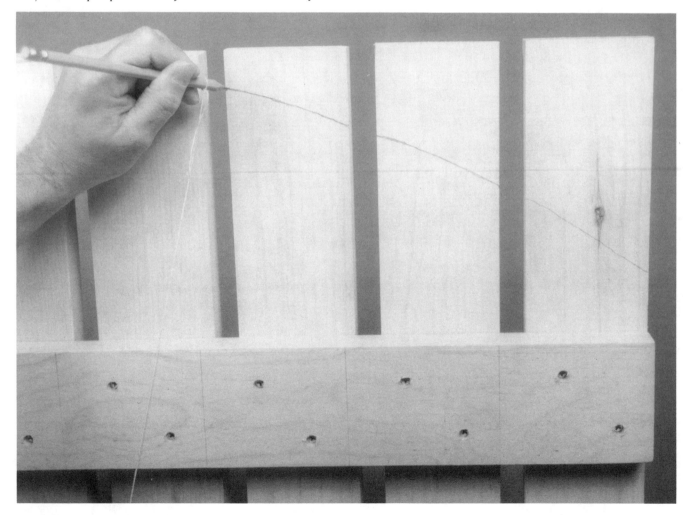

ONE CONSISTENT CURVE

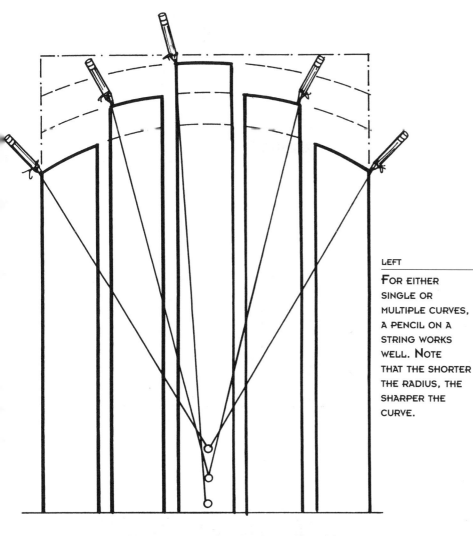

LEFT

FOR EITHER
SINGLE OR
MULTIPLE CURVES,
A PENCIL ON A
STRING WORKS
WELL. NOTE
THAT THE SHORTER
THE RADIUS, THE
SHARPER THE
CURVE.

FOR A CONSISTENT CURVE FROM ONE side of the slats to the other, you can draw this line simply by anchoring your string somewhere along the center slat. Experiment with different radius lengths. You'll find that a 30-inch radius creates a more subtle curve than a 20-inch radius. You may prefer to draw this arc on the back (rather than the face) of the chair or bench back, because you can make the string longer and anchor it below the seat, all the way to the base of the center slat.

Don't actually draw on the slats until you like the line a particular radius (string length) will produce. Of course you can sand off any line you don't like. But eyeball it before committing.

After you've drawn your line, you simply make the cut with your saber saw. Once you've made this cut, buff the end grain with a belt sander or palm sander, and your chair back is done.

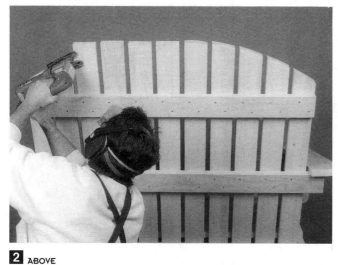

2 ABOVE

A JIGSAW IS THE PROPER TOOL FOR CUTTING ALONG CURVED LINES.

3 ABOVE

A BELT SANDER MAKES SHORT WORK OF ROUNDING, SMOOTHING, AND SHAPING THE BACK SLATS.

MULTIPLE CURVES

TO CREATE BACK SLATS THAT HAVE A NUMBER OF different curves, the ones where the back slats look "stepped," or "scalloped," you will use the same pencil-on-a-string technique. But this time move your anchor up or down the center back slat until you have a radius you want for each step. For instance, in the second and third back slat designs shown on this page, there are three different circles creating the stepped effect. The outer two slats are one circle's radius, the first slat in from either side is another circle's radius, and the center slat is its own circle.

The question is, which radius should you use? Typically, for the chair, the radius will range anywhere from 20 inches to 30 inches. By measuring down between 20 inches and 30 inches from the top of the center slat (and be sure the anchor is centered exactly in the middle of the center slat!), you will create subtle curves. The longer the radius, the more subtle the curve. A 20-inch radius, for instance, will give you a tighter, more pronounced arc than a longer radius, whose arc will be gentler. For the bench, you may have to use a radius longer than 30 inches; otherwise the circle won't span the full 4-foot bench width.

Here's a hint: To get the most consistent "stepped" look, vary the distance between your anchors by the same number of inches. For instance, if you draw your first circle with a 30-inch radius, draw your second circle with a 28-inch radius, your third circle with a 26-inch radius, and so on, subtracting 2 inches each time.

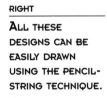

RIGHT

ALL THESE DESIGNS CAN BE EASILY DRAWN USING THE PENCIL-STRING TECHNIQUE.

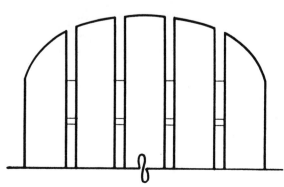

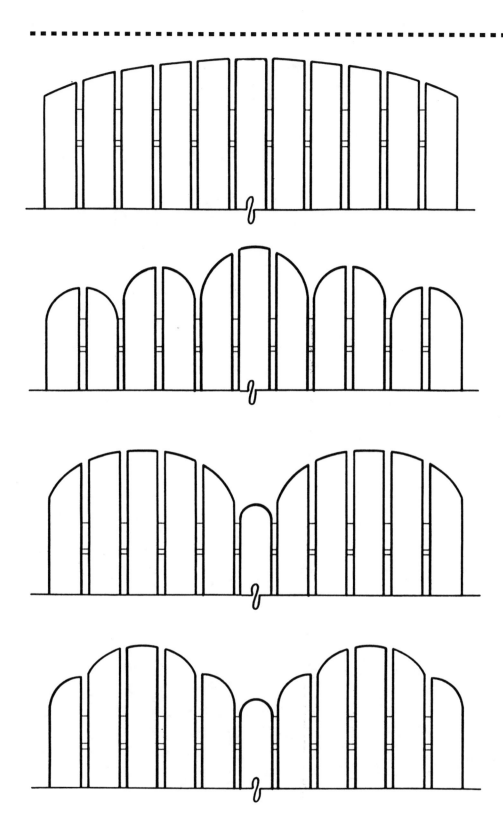

■THE FLORAL LOOK

To give your back slats a floral look, that can't be drawn by the string-pencil method, the best thing to do is to make a cardboard template and lay the template on each slat or pair of slats to draw the design. To make the template, get a piece of cardboard as wide as the slat (or slats) you will trace onto. Then, fold it exactly in half, and cut freehand with scissors or a craft knife. If you mess up, just start with another piece of cardboard. Once you get a template you like, you can use it as a master for making others.

■OTHER BACK-SLAT DESIGNS

Don't limit yourself to the designs suggested here. If you want to make up some other designs, or if you're inspired by motifs you see elsewhere, by all means, let your imagination fly. The marking and cutting techniques presented in this and other chapters may be helpful.

ABOVE

The wider back on the Adirondack bench allows for more elaborate designs.

FINISHING YOUR ADIRONDACK FURNITURE

THERE ARE THREE BASIC TYPES OF applied finish you can use on your Adirondack furniture: paint, sealant, or urethane.

If you've used a quality wood for the furniture, you really should seal or urethane it. There is no sense shelling out for quality wood and then covering it over with paint. Use a finish that enhances the grain and look of the wood while simultaneously protecting it against weather and sun. If you've used a lesser-quality wood (one, say, with lots of knots), paint may be your finish of choice. But before choosing any finish, look closely at the options and weigh their pros and cons.

ABOVE AND RIGHT

IF YOU CHOOSE TO PAINT YOUR CHAIR, USE EXTERIOR PAINT ONLY. PRIME THE CHAIR FIRST AND THEN APPLY AT LEAST TWO FINISH COATS.

■ OIL VS. LATEX

If you paint your chair, you will have a choice between latex or oil-based (alkyd) paint. If you can find it (some states have outlawed it), use oil-based paint. Reason: The solvent in oil-based paint won't swell the wood, and, though it takes longer to dry, oil-based paint leaves a slightly smoother, more consistent finish. It's a bit more expensive than latex, but since you'll only be using a quart or two, it's a small amount of money. As for cleanup, you'll have to use thinner, which adds a bit to the cost, too. (By the way, you can recycle paint thinner simply by letting it sit—the solids and paint settle out, it clears, and you can reuse it.)

Latex paint offers ease of use, a slightly cheaper price, and an adequate protective finish. Latex paint is *waterborne* rather than oil-borne, and when you apply it, the water affects the wood as any water would, swelling it slightly. It's not that big an issue, because we are not restoring Early American furniture for the Smithsonian here, we're painting a lawn chair. But it is the reason I would pick oil-based paint over latex. As for protective performance, when all is said and done, latex and oil-based paints will perform equally well.

No matter what kind of paint you choose, be sure it is *exterior paint*. Interior paint won't hold up well, even under normal weathering.

■ GLOSS VS. FLAT

Should you use flat, semi-gloss, or high gloss finish? I'd go for a semi-gloss or a high gloss. I certainly wouldn't use a flat-finish paint. It's unwashable, picks up stains easily, and won't weather the rain as well as a higher gloss. Also, flat paint is mildly abrasive and you won't be able to slide around on the chair as comfortably as with a high gloss paint. And some flat paints rub off on clothing, making them a liability when your mother-in-law in her white linen dress comes calling for high tea.

Semi-gloss, on the other hand, is washable, smooth, and weathers well. In bright sun, it won't be too glaring on the eyes, and, well, it just plain looks good. High gloss is perfectly good to use, but it might be a little too shiny for you. The choice between semi-gloss and high gloss is really a toss-up—ultimately a matter of taste.

■ PRIMED VS. UNPRIMED

If you paint, you should prime, no question about it. Primer provides a foundation for the top coat and will give the overall paint job a longer life. When you pick a primer, be sure that you match it to your finish coat. Some latex primers, for instance, cannot be used beneath oil-based finish coats. Ask at your paint store for a primer that's right for your finish coat.

Knots in wood will bleed their resins through paint. You have to prime knots with a special knot sealer. Some primers offer knot-sealing capability, but the best thing to do is use an alcohol-based primer called BIN or KILLSTAIN, (both trade names). These products are used to hide the kinds of things that keep bleeding through paint: smoke stains, water stains, children's magic marker doodles. They are very fast drying and don't smooth out the way oil-based paints will. So get them on fast and right. Apply either with a "suicide brush" (a $1 throwaway). Smooth it out with your brush as much as possible. Knot sealants are as thin as water at first, but they quickly gum up as they dry. Prime all knots thoroughly!

Sealing

SEALING THE FURNITURE WILL PRESERVE THE NATURAL grain of the wood. Plus, sealant offers the added benefit of protecting the wood against mildew, water, and the destructive ultraviolet rays of the sun. It's easy to apply, looks great, and is the protective coating I recommend for quality wood.

Sealants are available as water- or oil-based products. They typically soak into the wood, like traditional stain, preserving the wood's natural look. Sealants dry flat, and can be applied in multiple coats (usually the topmost coat is applied while the one beneath it is still tacky wet). Tung oil is a really good sealant, and I'd recommend that you put on at least three coats of it before setting your furniture out. Over the course of the first season, you want to coat the furniture a couple more times, then apply a coat once a year, or as needed.

If you seal the wood, there's no need to apply a polyurethane finish, though some sealants can be covered with polyurethane.

LEFT

TUNG OIL, APPLIED WITH A CLEAN, LINT-FREE, COTTON CLOTH, IS AN EXCELLENT WOOD FINISH. WEAR RUBBER GLOVES TO PROTECT YOUR SKIN.

IF YOU LIKE THE NATURAL FINISH OF YOUR WOOD, you can simply coat it with a polyurethane. Or, you can "stain and 'thane"—stain the wood to darken it, then coat it with polyurethane: Either way, polyurethane can offer good protection against water, mildew, and the sun. It's akin to coating your furniture with a thin layer of durable plastic.

Pick your polyurethane carefully, though. Make sure the polyurethane you buy has *ultraviolet protection*. The label on the can should say something like "exterior grade" or "UV resistant."

There are different finishes in polyurethane, from "satin" to "high gloss." So long as the polyurethane is exterior rated, the finish you choose is mostly a matter of taste. Your paint store should have some sample blocks painted with the different finishes.

Since you are going to be using so little polyurethane (probably a gallon *at most*), buy the best you can get. The work you save applying a long-lasting, high-quality product will quickly pay you back for the extra $5 you lay out at the store for a premium gallon.

When getting ready to apply the urethane, don't shake the can. That creates bubbles that won't easily settle out. Stir the can. Just before you apply a coat of urethane, you may want to vacuum the piece of furniture to remove any remaining sawdust. After you have applied a coat, let it dry thoroughly, and then buff it lightly with #220 sandpaper or steel wool. That will take down any burrs or grain that the first coat has brought up. Before applying another coat on top of a sanded coat, use a *tack cloth* to wipe down the furniture and remove any grit or dirt.

ABOVE

POLYURETHANE IS AN EXCELLENT PROTECTIVE COATING TO APPLY TO WOOD. USE AN EXTERIOR-RATED POLYURETHANE AND APPLY IT WITH A BRISTLE BRUSH.

MAKING BLOCKS FROM SCRAP 11

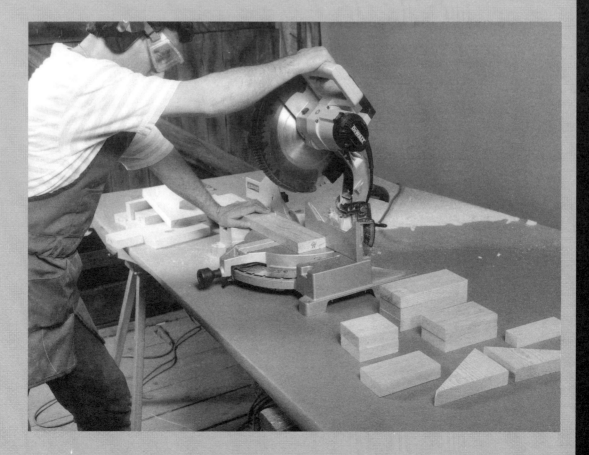

G OT SOME WOOD SCRAPS LEFT OVER? Since we've used quality wood for our furniture projects, these scraps can make a great block set for kids. Here is a cutting diagram that shows some of the pieces for a traditional block set. Of course, you can change the dimensions or the design as you see fit.

Square cuts can be made with a chop saw or a table saw. The cuts that run corner to corner can be made on a table saw or chop saw (be careful when ripping wood on a di- agonal!), and the curved cuts can be made with your jigsaw or saber saw.

Be sure to select the wood carefully and choose only the highest quality scrap—that is, wood that won't ever split. When you've made your cuts, sand the edges and end grains carefully so young fingers don't get splinters.

Mix and match the block designs so you have a good assortment of each shape. Just a couple of 16-inch blocks will do, but as any block builder knows, there is no such thing as too many 4- and 8-inch blocks.

BELOW

SHOWN HERE ARE SOME TRADITIONAL BLOCK SHAPES, BUT DON'T OVER- LOOK BUILDING THE ODD TRAPEZOID OR RHOMBUS. YOUNG BLOCK-BUILDERS WILL APPRECIATE THEM.

■ BASIC BLOCK SHAPES

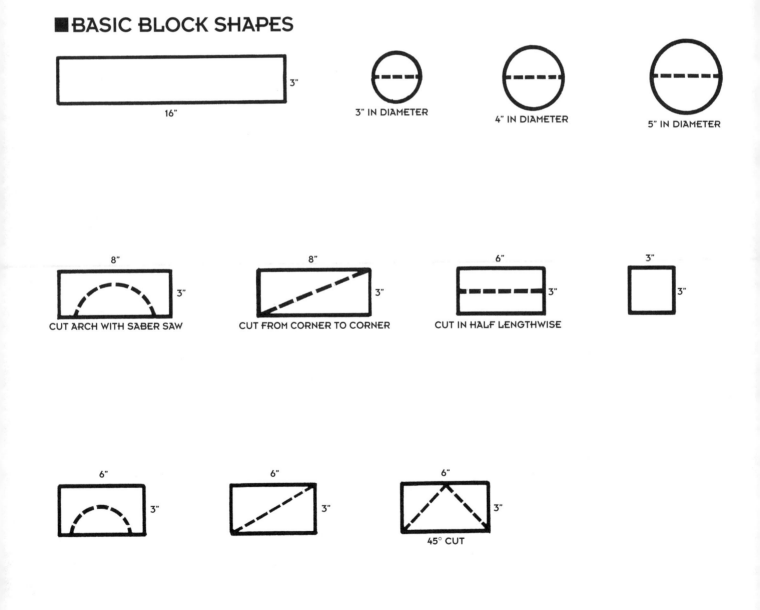

■BASIC MEASUREMENT EQUIVALENTS

inches	×	25.4	= millimeters	millimeters	×	.03937	= inches
feet	×	.3048	= meters	meters	×	3.2809	= feet
miles	×	1.6093	= kilometers	kilometers	×	.62138	= miles
square inches	×	6.4515	= square centimeters	square centimeters	×	.155	= square inches
square feet	×	.0929	= square meters	square meters	×	10.7641	= square feet
acres	×	.4047	= hectares	hectares	×	2.471	= acres
acres	×	.00405	= square kilometers	square kilometers	×	247.1098	= acres
cubic inches	×	16.3872	= cubic centimeters	cubic centimeters	×	.06103	= cubic inches
cubic feet	×	.02832	= cubic meters	cubic meters	×	35.314	= cubic feet
cubic yards	×	.76452	= cubic meters	cubic meters	×	1.308	= cubic yards
cubic inches	×	.01639	= liters	liters	×	61.023	= cubic inches
U. S. gallons	×	3.7854	= liters	liters	×	.26418	= U.S. gallons
ounces	×	28.35	= grams	grams	×	.03527	= ounces
pounds	×	.4536	= kilograms	kilograms	×	2.2046	= pounds
ton (2000 lbs.)	×	.9072	= metric tons (1000 kg.)	metric tons (1000 kg.)	×	1.1023	= tons (2000 lbs.)
lbs. per sq. in. (PSI)	×	.0703	= kg.'s per sq. cm.	kg.'s per sq. cm.	×	14.2231	= lbs. per sq. in. (PSI)

■FRACTIONS AND DECIMALS

$1/32$ = .03125	$9/32$ = .28125	$17/32$ = .53125	$25/32$ = .78125
$1/6$ = .0625	$5/16$ = .3125	$9/16$ = .5625	$13/16$ = .8125
$3/32$ = .09375	$11/32$ = .34375	$19/32$ = .59375	$27/32$ = .84375
$1/8$ = .125	$3/8$ = .375	$5/8$ = .625	$7/8$ = .875
$5/32$ = .15625	$13/32$ = .40625	$21/32$ = .65625	$29/32$ = .90625
$3/16$ = .1875	$7/16$ = .4375	$11/16$ = .6875	$15/16$ = .9375
$7/32$ = .21875	$15/32$ = .46875	$23/32$ = .71875	$31/32$ = .96875
$1/4$ = .25	$1/2$ = .5	$3/4$ = .75	1 = 1.000

INDEX